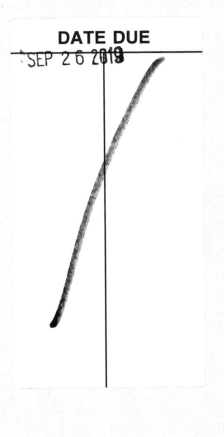
HOW DARE THE SUN RISE

HOW DARE THE SUN RISE

MEMOIRS OF A WAR CHILD

SANDRA UWIRINGIYIMANA

WITH ABIGAIL PESTA

KT KATHERINE TEGEN BOOKS
An Imprint of HarperCollins Publishers

Photographs courtesy of Sandra Uwiringiyimana

Gatumba survivor portraits courtesy of Sandra Uwiringiyimana
and Alex Ngabo

Katherine Tegen Books is an imprint of HarperCollins Publishers.

www.epicreads.com

Library of Congress Control Number: 2016957991
ISBN 978-0-06-247014-0 (hardback) — ISBN 978-0-06-247015-7 (pbk.)

Typography by Ray Shappell

18 19 20 21 22   PC/LSCH   10 9 8 7 6 5 4 3

❖

First Edition

THIS BOOK IS FOR YOU, MOM AND DAD.
TO YOU, DEBORAH, AND THE 165 ANGELS.

IKI GITABO NGITUYE MAMA NA PAPA.
NGITUYE DEBORAH NABAZIRA KARENGANE 165.

HOW DARE THE SUN RISE

ONE

THE NIGHT BEGAN SOFTLY. MY LITTLE SISTER, Deborah, and I were lying in bed, closing our eyes, trying to fall asleep in the midsummer heat. It was a couple hours past dark, a scorcher of an August evening in Africa. I could hear the soothing voices of my mother and aunt, chatting outdoors in the still, heavy air. Deborah was six years old at the time, and I had just turned ten. For some reason, Deborah had been highly sentimental that day, hugging my mother and me, telling us she loved us. She did it time and again. I wondered what had come over her.

Perhaps, somehow, she sensed that she would soon be leaving us.

Sleep did not come that night. My mother stormed in from outside, a look of panic on her face like I had never seen. Mom was always such a calm, wise presence, strong and rarely rattled. At the time, we were living as refugees, driven from our home in the Democratic Republic of the Congo because we belonged to a minority tribe, the Banyamulenge. For the past three months, I had been sleeping on a mattress on the ground in a big green tent at a crowded refugee camp in Burundi run by the refugee arm of the United Nations. I shared my mattress with Mom and Deborah, the youngest of my six sisters and brothers. Mom and my sister Princesse lived in our tent too. My dad and my brothers Alex and Heritage stayed in a tent next to ours. My sister Adele and brother Chris were with my grandparents, up high in the Congolese mountains known as the Hauts Plateaux.

We were scattered, an unsettling feeling in such an uncertain time. For weeks I had been dreaming of home—our big yellow-brick house with a grass-green roof, filled with cousins and friends. I longed for the sparkling blue waters of Lake Tanganyika, the colossal lake where I loved to swim, despite my parents' warnings about crocodiles. In the refugee camp, I had been imagining a time when I could return to school. I was an ace student, and I wanted desperately to put on my school uniform—navy-blue knee-length skirt, white button-down polo shirt, white socks—and get back to class. I thought surely we would be going home soon, and my family would all be together again.

That was wishful thinking.

Mom shook Deborah and me from the mattress where we slept. Princesse was away for the night, attending a choir concert in a nearby city.

"Mubyuke twatewe!" Mom said. "Wake up! We are under attack!"

We shared our tent with six families, mostly women and children. We knew one another intimately, like family. When people heard my mom's warning, they said, "No, you must be wrong. You're overreacting." Perhaps some thieves were stealing livestock from the nearby farm, they said, explaining away the distant sound of gunshots.

"No," my mother said. And then we saw my aunt, Nyarukundo. She had been hit by gunfire while standing outside the tent. Both of her arms had been struck, and one had nearly been ripped from the socket. That arm dangled oddly from her body, dark blood gushing like a river.

"We need to wrap her arm!" Mom said. "Help me find something to wrap it with."

I was surprised that my mother knew what to do in such a situation. It would have made sense to use my bedsheet.

I had seen enough action films with my brothers to know that sheets were the go-to item in that situation, but I couldn't think. I couldn't see well either, as the tent was dark as night. I opened my suitcase and grabbed a favorite silky blue dress that made me feel like a princess. The dress was brand new, the most important and beautiful thing I owned. I had been thinking of wearing it to church that Sunday, but I was afraid to get it dirty—church was held outside, in the middle of the camp, and we all sat on the ground. I thrust the dress at Mom. Now I wasn't worried about soiling it; I just wanted to help my aunt. But the material was too slippery to wrap her blood-soaked arm. My mother pulled off the inner layer of her traditional cotton dress and used that instead.

We heard noise approaching rapidly as men descended on the camp by foot, gunshots piercing the night. The shots sounded like popping corn at first, then grew louder as they came near. The tent erupted in chaos. People began shouting directions.

"Cut a hole in the side of the tent!" someone yelled. "We'll escape through there!"

People started huddling together in a corner. Somebody stepped on my leg, sending a rush of pain through my body. "Ow!" I said. But nobody heard. Everyone was in a panic.

Someone cut the hole in the tent, and a stream of people ran out, including one of my cousins, Jeanette.

Those people were gunned down, one by one, as they fled into the night. This isn't real, I thought. There is no way this is happening. I must be having a terrible dream. Surely I will wake up and it will all go away.

Mom grabbed my sister, my aunt, and me, along with two of my little cousins, Musore and Rusengo, who were six and nine years old. Mom said to hide beneath a mattress, and so we covered ourselves with the bed, staying close together, tense and still, down low to the ground. My aunt was in agony. The mattress was thin, and I thought about how bullets can so easily penetrate mattresses. It didn't make sense to hide beneath bedding from men with guns. But where else were we to go?

I wondered if my dad and brothers were safe. I heard our attackers singing and chanting. They were singing Christian songs. I had grown up singing some of those songs in church, and I wondered why murderers would be singing them.

"Imana yabatugabiye," the men chanted. "God has given you to us."

The men seemed to think they were on a mission from God to massacre us. They spoke in two languages from the region, Kirundi and Swahili. I spoke both languages, and their voices sounded familiar. Why were we being targeted by people who were praising God? Gunshots, screams, chanting. Nothing made sense. It didn't register that people were dying, that my cousin had been shot dead as she ran from the tent.

We must have been under the mattress for half an hour, huddled in silence. I didn't cry. I thought Mom would somehow find a way to protect us, because that's what mothers do.

I heard splashes hitting the tent all around us. I thought it was beginning to rain. The sound of rain was always loud in the tent, as the raindrops pelted the tarp like little torpedoes.

Then I heard a distant roar—fire. It sounded like it was burning through other tents.

The chanting grew louder and closer.

"God has given you to us. God has given you to us."

Suddenly there was a moment of stillness outside our tent. Maybe the men were leaving since it had started raining, I thought. There were just a few of us left in the tent, so perhaps they didn't care. They had killed everyone else. Maybe they were done.

Then we noticed the sharp fumes of kerosene. It had not begun to rain, after all: The tent had been doused in kerosene. We continued to hide, paralyzed, until we heard some men come to the entrance of the tent.

"Is anyone still here?" they called. "We've come to rescue you."

At first we stayed quiet. And then I heard my mother say, "Have you really come to help us?"

I had a panicked feeling. I didn't trust these men, even if they did speak our language. I had seen a lot of Jean-Claude Van Damme movies with my brothers—I knew that if these men were bad guys, they were not going to tell us.

"Come outside," the men said. "We will lead you to safety."

My mother seemed to believe them. I guess she felt she had no alternative but to trust them—what else could she do? Our tent would soon be in flames.

"Follow me," she said. She carried Deborah on her back and gripped the hands of my two young cousins on either side. My aunt crawled along beside her, somehow still conscious despite the loss of blood. I stayed a few steps behind, wary. I worried that Mom was being too trusting.

It was pitch black. I extended my arms to feel my way through the narrow "hallway" of the tent. I held on to the thick logs that propped up the tent, telling myself that each log could bring me a step closer to freedom. The shadows of the men loomed in the doorway. I heard a voice in my head saying: *Don't go. Stay back.* But I needed to stick with my mother, even if I doubted the intentions of those men. I couldn't leave Mom. We had to stay together. Still, I remained a few feet back, as the hallway wasn't wide enough for all six of us.

Mom came to a stop at the door of the tent. She stood there, waiting to be saved, as promised. I was finally close enough to see the faces of the men who said they would deliver us from this hell. Their eyes glowed in the fiery light, their backs to the flames. They looked young, perhaps in their twenties. I began to feel a sense of relief: Maybe they really would help us, after all. They wore camouflage pants and hats, military-style clothes. I could see their shoulders bulging from their tank tops, shining with sweat. One of the men carried a giant roll of bullets, like you'd see in action movies. The other carried a machine gun. They looked at us.

"Bashiriremo!" one of them barked. "Shoot them!"

Suddenly, I saw sparks—bright blasts of gunfire—hitting my mother. They looked like fireworks. The bullets went into her belly, and she crumpled. She was still carrying my sister on her back. I turned around and ran inside the tent. I didn't want to leave my mom—children are supposed to run toward their mothers for protection, not away from them. But I had seen the sparks. I knew that I had to hide.

With my arms stretched wide to feel my way through the hallway, careful not to run into the logs, I stumbled back to my mattress refuge. I kept seeing sparks fly in front of me. A future as an orphan flashed before my eyes.

I prayed to God. "If you keep my parents alive, I will be good," I promised. At the same time, I knew my mother had just been gunned down. She must be dead. Deborah must be dead too. My little six-year-old sister, gone. That beautiful girl who brushed the sand from my skin after my secret swims in the lake. Gone. I couldn't accept the thought of it. She and my mother could not leave me. They simply couldn't. I kept praying. I begged God to please let us all survive.

"I'll never tell a lie," I said. "I'll always do what my mom tells me."

Then I blacked out.

I awoke when something hot hit my leg. A fiery piece of tent had fallen from above and burned through the mattress, scorching my skin. The tent was in flames. Everything was melting around me. I saw men stealing things from our suitcases, grabbing whatever they could. They didn't notice me. I felt like I was in a movie scene—a ten-year-old girl sitting in the center of the frame, while war raged around her.

The men left, and I called for my mother. I called and called in the dark.

"Mom! Mom!"

I knew my mom would never abandon me. But I knew what I had seen, the sparks that sent her to the ground.

The smoke began to choke me, and I needed to run. I managed to crash my way through the burning debris of the tent. I emerged in the decimated camp, standing for a moment, frozen. Limbs, bones, and bloody bodies lay everywhere. I smelled burning flesh. I saw men with guns, machetes, torches. They were marching around the camp, looking for survivors to kill. They slashed my people with their machetes. They set my people on fire. They shot my people in the head. Tents were ablaze. A man was being burned alive across the camp, screaming in agony on his knees. I learned later that he was a beloved pastor who had led the prayers in the camp every morning before the sun rose. I had listened to him preach while sitting on the damp, dewy grass with my mom and little sister. On chilly mornings, I would curl up close to Mom, snuggling beneath her cotton wrap while the pastor led us in prayer, and Deborah would sleep in Mom's lap. Now this man was on fire.

People fled for a nearby farm. But before I could run, a man grabbed me by the shirt. He looked at me and I looked at him.

"Mbabarira," I said. "Forgive me."

I don't know why I said it. I suppose at ten years old, I thought I must have done something terribly wrong to bring on such wrath. My parents had always taught me to be polite and to apologize when I did something wrong. The man pointed a gun to my head.

I felt the metal barrel on my temple. I waited for the blast. In that moment, I thought it was all over.

"Good-bye, life," I said.

TWO

TEN YEARS BEFORE THE FLAMES, I WAS BORN in the mountains, a scenic land of jewel-green fields, bamboo trees, and forests inhabited by gorillas, elephants, and chimpanzees. My people lived in small round mud huts with pointy roofs made of dried grass. They raised cattle and farmed the land. My parents grew up in these towering mountains, the Hauts Plateaux, in a province of the Democratic Republic of the Congo called South Kivu. When they were young, my mom and dad lived in neighboring villages that were about a day apart by foot. There were no roads, no cars. Everyone walked everywhere, and they still do.

We left the mountains when I was around two years old,

in 1996, so I don't remember much of our life there. But today when I see pictures of the region, known as Minembwe, it looks like the most idyllic place on earth, with lush, leafy mountaintops scraping the clouds and miles and miles of green. People still live in mud houses with grass roofs there. Smoke from burning wood lingers in the air.

My parents met for the first time on the day of their wedding—an arranged marriage. Whenever I ask them about it, they describe it very matter-of-factly. It's not as if they had a courtship or romance. At the time, my mom was just fourteen years old. She had completed five years of school, which was considered a lot of education for a girl in those days. Typically, after five or six years of school, girls simply dropped out, because there seemed to be no point in continuing their education: Their fate was to marry young and produce children. My dad was eighteen years old, just finishing high school. Schools were sparse in the mountains, and he walked for miles each day to get that education.

One day toward the end of his senior year, my dad came home from final exams and his father announced that he had found him a bride. My dad had never seen this mysterious young wife-to-be. He knew only that she was from another village and had a few years of schooling—a fact that worried his own father, who thought that was too much education for a woman. My father was not worried about this at all. He was intrigued by the idea of an educated woman.

To arrange a wedding in my culture, the man's family gives the woman's family a dowry, usually a number of cows in exchange for the woman's hand. My father's family negotiated a deal to give my mother's family ten cows. Then the families talked to a local pastor, who checked that both sides had consented to the union. For my young parents, it wasn't really up to them. It's just the way things were done. So, of course, they consented.

The two married in a low-key affair in a church, more like a business arrangement than a romantic wedding, although my mother's bridesmaids did pamper her in the days beforehand, slathering her with lotions, making sure she looked beautiful. People in the villages created everything by hand, including a skin lotion made from milk oil. To make the lotion, women would fill jugs with milk and shake the jugs until the fat separated from the milk. That fat would be turned into oil that made a rich cream for skin, and could also be used for cooking. The jugs were handmade too—created from hollowed-out gourds.

My parents made a striking pair of newlyweds, both tall and good-looking, my mom with a stately, confident air, and my dad, soft-spoken, gentle, and sincere, with an easy smile and a long, straight nose. For the wedding, Mom wore a traditional African dress—long and formfitting, in shades of blue and purple—and Dad wore a classic dress shirt and pants. After the ceremony, my mother's relatives hiked back to their village and left her with her new husband and his family in their village. My mom knew no one there, not even her own husband. To a fourteen-year-old girl—a child bride—it must have felt like she was a world away.

Then it was my mom's job to get pregnant. That was a woman's duty: to marry and bear children. But her young body wasn't ready to carry a child. She had two miscarriages, and people began to whisper, saying that if she couldn't have children, it must be due to witchcraft. Her in-laws shunned her for not performing her job. My mother had a very difficult time in those early years of marriage; she was a teenage girl, ostracized by the adults around her. But she was also very strong willed, determined to rise above the people who made her feel small.

In time, she managed to give birth to my oldest brother, Heritage. After that, she began having a child every couple years or so. I was the sixth. In my culture, having a lot of kids was a symbol of health and wealth, unless the children were all girls. Girls were basically seen as useless. This has always struck me as odd. The women in our culture are known for working incredibly hard, juggling so many things—raising the children, working on the farm, harvesting, fetching and chopping firewood, and then cooking dinner for the men. Traditionally, the women prepare the meals and the husbands eat alone, or with their male friends, not with their wives. It makes me cringe, but that is the culture.

A couple years after I was born, my family left the mountains amid one of the many conflicts in the region and moved to a city in the valley below, Uvira. The city is known for its beauty—the glistening Lake Tanganyika, the winding Kalimabenge River—and also for its conflicts. War was part of our everyday life.

There was always a new rebellion, a new battle. There are hundreds of different tribes in Congo. My people, the Banyamulenge, have long been discriminated against and targeted in the region. Much of our early history is from word of mouth. I learned about it over the years from my parents, who told stories of our roots when I asked about various conflicts and wars. They had heard the tales from their own parents. They explained that in the late 1800s, many members of my tribe began moving from their native Rwanda to the mountains of South Kivu, a Congolese province. The tribe migrated for several reasons, including civil war and discrimination at home, as well as the fact that the mountains held an abundance of grasslands—a paradise for grazing cows. My people are famous for cattle farming. We are known for being a strong, strapping group, healthy from drinking lots of milk straight from the cow.

My tribe's migration came amid the time of European colonialism, and life was violent and turbulent across the region, as Africans were seized as slaves and forced into hard labor. Eventually, in 1960, the Congolese won a bloody battle for independence from Belgium. But the region was left deeply unstable, and civil wars raged. My people in South Kivu ran into political problems because they lived in a Congolese province but spoke a language of their native Rwanda. My people looked different, sounded different. They tried to keep to themselves. And so they were seen as foreigners. The Congolese didn't know where my tribe stood. Different groups vying for power would come after my people to get them to fight for one side or another, and chaos reigned. Over the decades, the Banyamulenge got caught up in various conflicts and civil wars, but no matter what, they were always seen as outsiders, not truly Congolese. We were—and still are—stateless. So many of my people today are languishing in refugee camps, belonging to no country, always in limbo.

My parents grew up amid these conflicts, and were sometimes forced from their homes and villages. During my own childhood, the battles continued, and I was always aware of them. It seemed like the norm.

For the most part, I loved my childhood in the city of Uvira. I often think back to its beauty—the warm summer sun shining down on the sparkling lake, the towering blue-gray mountains in the distance, and the ancient, shady mango tree in our neighborhood that people used as a guidepost when giving directions: "Turn left at the mango tree."

Things seemed simple then. I knew my parents loved me, and I felt safe with them. People I meet now assume that my childhood years in Africa were dark and deprived. But they were the opposite.

One of my most vivid early memories is of my little sister, Deborah. I was around four years old when she was born, and I remember this tiny, squirmy baby girl with a big, beautiful Afro of soft curls appearing in our home. Studying her face, I thought: Who are you? Where did you come from? I knew my mother had been pregnant, her belly protruding more by the day, but I was so young, I couldn't put it all together. I just remember Deborah suddenly arriving, and my mom making baby food, mashing together bananas and avocados by hand. I would sometimes steal a bite of the sweet, soft mixture, and my mom would shoo me away. It took me some time to understand that Deborah was truly ours and that we could keep her.

Until Deborah came, I had been the youngest. I had five older brothers and sisters—my brother Heritage, followed by my sister Princesse, my brother Chris, my sister Adele, my brother Alex, and then me.

In our tribe, parents give their kids both a first and last name—family members don't share a last name. My father's name is Prudence Munyakuri. My mother's name is Rachel Namberwa. My siblings are Heritage Munyakuri, Princesse Nabintu, Christian Ntagawa, Adele Kibasumba, Alex Ngabo, and Deborah Mukobgajana. Parents typically choose names with a goal of helping to shape their children's character. I was named after a Rwandan prime minister, Agathe Uwiringiyimana, an influential woman in the history of Rwanda. I love that my parents named me after her. It makes me feel like I have big shoes to fill, and that someday I can do something worth being remembered for—although, let's not kid anyone, my last name is way too long, and I don't wish that on any other child. My last name means "one who believes in God," another aspect of my name that helps define me.

Alex and I were the closest in age among my siblings, and we always played together, and got into trouble together—usually his fault. He was a small kid, funny and mischievous, a bit of a troublemaker. I called him my "little brother," even though he was older than me. He taught me tomboyish things, like how to do a handstand: He would hold my legs up against the wall to keep me steady as I stood on my hands, then he would start to let go and freak me out. He taught me to play soccer with his friends, using makeshift balls made from wadded-up plastic bags and rubber bands. We played in a dusty alleyway, with brick walls on either side, where there wasn't much parental traffic. We were always getting scrapes and scratches.

One time, my shorts ripped when I fell and my butt was showing, but I knew not to cry. Alex wouldn't allow it, probably because he didn't want to get in trouble if I went home in tears. Instead, I considered my ripped shorts a badge of honor; I was like one of the boys.

Alex also taught me how to ride a bike, or at least he tried. It was an adult bike that was too big for me, so I couldn't keep it under control. We weren't supposed to be riding it at all. It was my mom's bike, and she used it to run errands and go to the market. One day, Alex decided it would be a good idea for both of us to get on the bike and ride down a steep, fast hill. I trusted my brother so much that I would have ridden that bike blindfolded. I wanted his approval—I wanted him to think I was cool—and so I hopped on.

"Hold on tight!" he said. We flew down the hill, but couldn't keep the bike stable, and we crashed. I got scraped up pretty badly.

"Don't tell Mom," Alex begged me. "She'll kill me." And so I didn't tell. I still have scars on my arms and knees.

It was a typical scenario with Alex. But he also had the purest heart. One night, he thought he heard people talking outside of our home in the dark. He feared they were burglars who would come and find us in our beds. He poked me to wake me up.

"We need to pray," he said. "We need to pray to protect our family."

"We're fine," I told him. "The wind is probably carrying people's voices from somewhere else." But he insisted that I pray to God with him, to help make the prayers stronger. I got up and we prayed together.

I had a different kind of relationship with my older sisters. I idolized them. Princesse was seven years older than me, and Adele was five years older. I wanted to wear clothes like them. I wanted to hang out with them and their friends. If my mom made skirts or dresses for them, I wanted the same ones. I would look at their new outfits and say, "Mom! What about me?"

Princesse was elegant and ladylike, at least on the surface.

Underneath, she was more like a rebel, a tomboy. She wore pants and T-shirts into her teens, which you weren't supposed to do once you were a teenager. It was okay when you were a little girl, but as you grew up, you were supposed to wear dresses and make yourself into marriage material. She also had a quirky sense of humor and loved to clown around; I remember her cracking up at fart jokes during dinner. Mom would usually laugh. Dad would eye us, unamused. Yet Princesse was also very responsible: She often helped Mom take care of us younger kids, getting us bathed and into bed at night. If Princesse told me to do something, I would do it.

With Adele, who was a little closer in age to me, it was different: If she told me to do something, I would snap back, "You're not my mother." Still, I wanted to be like her. She was outgoing, dynamic, and stylish, with a lot of friends. She and her friends often got into gossipy tangles, and she was always in a cool clique. She grew tall quickly, with long limbs that made her awkward as a child. She was not the most coordinated dancer, but she was strikingly pretty.

My brother Chris was handsome and shy, a sweet, skinny kid with the greatest smile in the world. Like my brother Alex, he looked out for me. Unlike Alex, he seemed proud of me. Alex was a little too close to me in age for that. Chris would often take me to a little kiosk down the street, where a man sold things like matches, candles, and candy. We would hang out there and buy little things. Sometimes Chris would mind the kiosk himself if the man needed a break. When Chris took over, he always gave me candy.

As a young girl, I never knew my oldest brother, Heritage. Congolese soldiers snatched him from our home in Uvira when he was in grade school and I was too young to remember. Armed soldiers approached and grabbed him so they could force him to serve in the army. My dad begged the soldiers to take him instead of Heritage, arguing that his son was too young, but they didn't listen.

It was typical at the time for soldiers to kidnap boys— they would seize kids and brainwash them, training them to do unthinkable things, then send them out to different regions of the country. I have vivid memories of seeing young kids in the streets of Uvira holding guns bigger than themselves. On the day the soldiers grabbed Heritage, they seized around two hundred kids. Imagine being a child and being whisked away from your home by violent strangers. My parents didn't know if they would ever see Heritage again. But from that day, my father vowed to find his son and bring him home. I wondered if I would ever know my oldest brother.

As my sister Deborah grew, I began teaching her the same kinds of athletic things that Alex had taught me, like how to do handstands. We shared girly things too, like our collection of soft fabric dolls that we would dress with outfits we concocted from cloth remnants. Sometimes we would get bright scraps of fabric from dresses Mom had made. Other times, we would go to the tailor and ask for leftover fabrics. He always handed them over. Our dolls were lumpy and amorphous, fun to cuddle up with in bed.

All of us kids shared bedrooms, and Deborah and I began sharing a bed when she was a few years old. At night before bedtime, we all took turns brushing our teeth, but when money was tight and we couldn't afford toothpaste, my mom told us to brush with coal. We rubbed it on our teeth, then rinsed. The nights were hot and steamy, as we had no air-conditioning. I didn't even know that there was such a thing.

We went to sleep to a cacophony of crickets, their chirps floating through the windows. We lay on mattresses with mosquito nets draped overhead. The nets hung from the ceiling, and we tucked them in under the mattresses each night. Our windows had netting to keep the mosquitoes out as well, but the pests still managed to find their way in. Dad would sometimes give us shots to prevent malaria. We would have to lie down on the bed and get the shot in our butts—and that shot really hurt.

I'll never forget those nights with Deborah. She was such

a loyal little sister. She was so beautiful, it was almost unfair. She had wonderfully thick, black curly hair. My mother brushed it every day, but you couldn't really tell that she had brushed it because the curls always kept their form. Deborah could walk through a tornado and still come out with her curls intact. I was envious of her hair because mine was coarse and harder to maintain.

Deborah had big, soulful brown eyes that could light the whole world. We used to make fun of her when she would cry: We said she could produce a bucket of tears, her eyes were so big. And she had long, thick eyelashes that were the key to my parents' hearts. When we needed their permission to do something, we often sent Deborah to ask. If I wanted to play with my friends, I would tell Deborah that she could come and play with the little sisters of my friends—if Mom would let us. So then she would go and ask Mom. There was just something about Deborah that my parents couldn't say no to. I think it's because no one wanted to see her cry; her eyes were just too pretty.

Deborah was my constant companion, calm and thoughtful, like my dad. I was more stubborn and feisty, like my mom. Deborah knew all of my secrets. I was always instructing her not to tell on me if I did something bad, and she never did. I could trust her. She wanted me to like her, just like I had longed for Alex's approval when I was her age. She never betrayed me.

We were all very respectful of our parents. If we talked back, we got a spanking. But my parents were more gentle than strict. If my dad was unhappy with me, he would sit me down and calmly explain why. He would start by saying in his wise, deep voice, "You see, Sandra . . ." And then he would logically outline what I had done wrong.

We did, however, often defy our parents by going swimming. The Kalimabenge River, which separated the mountains from the city, was not far from our house, and we spent a lot of time there. We washed our dishes and clothes in the river, and then jumped in the water in our underwear. After swimming, we sat on boulders and collected smooth pebbles to juggle in the air. We also liked to swim in nearby Lake Tanganyika, one of the biggest lakes in the world. Our parents were always warning us not to swim.

"You could get malaria," Mom would say.

"You could drown."

"You could get eaten by crocodiles."

None of these possibilities ever stopped us.

Sometimes we would sneak away from home, quietly climbing the dark-green gate in our front yard and jumping over it so our parents wouldn't hear it creak. We would spend hours in the sunbaked water, emerging with skin so tight it felt like if you smiled, your face would crack. Our skin would look ashy from the residue, a telltale sign that we had been swimming. To wipe away the ashy evidence, we would rub ourselves with lotion or Vaseline before we returned home. Deborah would always be waiting for me outside our gate with the Vaseline. She rubbed it all over my body, making sure she got every spot so I wouldn't get in trouble.

I knew she longed for the day when she could swim with us.

THREE

I HAVE MAGICAL MEMORIES OF OUR HOME IN Uvira, before we lost my sister to war. We had a big African palm tree inside our front gate, and in the backyard, a banana tree and my favorite tree, called a madammé tree. It produced a fruit I loved—like a mango, rough and green on the outside, with reddish-yellow flesh on the inside, tart and sweet. My brother Alex taught me how to climb the tree to get more fruit, and, of course, I fell out of the tree.

I remember Deborah sitting beneath the tree, looking up at us in the branches. She was not big enough to climb, but you could see the desire in her eyes. She wanted to be up there with me.

"Come, I'll lift you up!" I would call to her.

"Oh no, you won't!" Mom would yell from the kitchen window.

One of my favorite memories is of my pet monkey, Kiki, a playful little fellow who was about as tall as my knees and followed me everywhere. Deborah loved Kiki too, but she was so young, she didn't understand that she shouldn't tease him with bananas. She would show him a banana and playfully yank it back, and they would get into these banana fights, pushing and pulling the fruit back and forth. That never ended well.

Our big yellow house was kid heaven. It was so roomy that we could play hide-and-seek with our friends indoors without annoying the adults. The house was one story, with high ceilings, a living room lined with cushy gray sofas, and a big dining room with a long wooden table. Deborah and I would eat our meals sitting directly on the table because we were too short to sit in the chairs. We had all the modern conveniences—electricity, running water, indoor plumbing, a bathtub, and a small stove. We didn't have hot running water. No one in our neighborhood did. It never even occurred to me that you could have hot water coming from the faucet. We didn't need it: It was almost always warm outside, and if the nights got chilly,

Mom would heat up the water for our baths.

My parents weren't wealthy. They moved into the house when they came down from the mountains, as the house had simply been abandoned. Many homes in Uvira had been left empty by families fleeing the conflicts that plagued the area. The homes belonged to no one. My parents saw it as a temporary living situation, and began building a house of their own. But in the meantime, that yellow house became home.

We had a radio, and I remember an educational UNICEF program for kids about different topics, like HIV. We also had a television, which was rare at that time. Dad was always calling Alex to adjust the antenna to get the best reception. Alex was small, the perfect height to fiddle with the antenna.

"Move it to the left," Dad would direct him from the sofa.

"Try to the right."

"Wait."

"Hold it. Try it there."

Alex would oblige, but not without rolling his eyes.

I watched soccer, cartoons, music shows featuring British boy bands, and world music from Ireland, America, Burundi. There was a Saturday program called *Au-delà du Son*—Beyond the Sound—which featured music from all over the world. This was the only way we knew which American songs were trending. Nelly, R. Kelly, Destiny's Child, Westlife, and Céline

Dion were among the Western artists we liked. I could sing Nelly and Kelly Rowland's "Dilemma" word for word, but I had no idea what the words meant. The same went for any R. Kelly or Céline Dion song.

As for Congolese music, I was the best dancer in the house, and I made sure everyone knew it. I danced the popular hip-swinging Ndombolo dance step by step, without missing a beat, starting at the age of five. I wasn't afraid to perform for anyone willing to watch me.

I also watched the soccer World Cup with great interest; I loved the game. My team was Brazil, and when my guys lost to France in 1998, I cried my eyes out. My parents and siblings all laughed at me because I was such a passionate fan.

My parents sheltered me from many of the civil war images that surfaced on TV. I didn't really understand war, because my parents did such a good job protecting me from it. I did understand the need to be safe. I did not understand why people would want to target us. Some days, I would eavesdrop on conversations among my parents and other adults. I would hear them talking about war that was either going on at the time or that was about to start. That's how I knew if we were likely to flee soon. Sometimes I caught a glimpse of my father opening a closet that he kept locked at all times, and for a good reason—there were several guns in there. I didn't understand why Dad owned guns; he was not a soldier, and I had never seen him shoot anything. I know now that he wanted to protect us from war, but at the time, I figured he was keeping them for an uncle in the military.

I had two uncles in the military, and they would often stop by the house with their friends to visit. I loved all of them dearly. They used to play with me and let me touch the stars adorning their uniforms. My favorite uncle was my mom's younger brother Rumenge. My mother loved him deeply too. He was a tall, handsome man, like a movie star. He was kind and gentle; it was hard to picture him as a soldier. He was always playing and laughing with me. He brought me gifts whenever he visited—candy, money, clothes—and I cried when he had to leave. I never knew what his job was in the military. Just like my father, he never explained why he had a gun.

For all I knew, our life was normal. I was a happy kid.

To be sure, there were daily challenges. The electricity went off all the time, at random hours throughout the day and night. When it happened, you could hear the neighborhood erupt in one big, heavy groan. Then kids would go out in the streets and sell petrol to light oil lamps.

"Petroleeeee!" they would call in a singsongy voice from the streets. "Petrol here!"

"Kuya apa!" we would reply. "Come here!"

The back-and-forth chant would continue until the kids found the customer. If people weren't interested in buying the petrol, the kids would sometimes snap at them, telling them to drink it: "Kunywa ayo!"

When the electricity came back on, you could hear the neighborhood cheer and clap.

My father was often away in those early years, working at different jobs to support the family, including a job in customs and immigration at the port. During this time, my uncle Rumenge became like a second father to me, visiting often. The doors of our home were always open to uncles, aunts, cousins, friends, visitors. There were at least three cousins staying with us at any given time. Privacy was not something that I knew. People came and went, all day long. No one bothered to knock on the door; they just wandered in.

The same went for traveling members of our tribe: Whenever they hiked down from the mountains and crossed the river to get to the city, our house was the first one they saw. They would often come and stay, to rest on their journey. It took about three days by foot to get from the mountains to the city. Our house was like a landmark: People knew to look for the big yellow house with the green roof. Mom would invite them in and lay out blankets for them to sleep on the living-room floor. They could stay as long as they liked.

Mom was like a saint, friendly to everyone in the neighborhood, including the homeless, the troubled, random drifters. Everyone knew her by name, even the most obscure outcasts—a lady with swollen feet and a cloud of flies around her, a strange drooling man with a lisp. They would show up at our front gate and my mom would give them food.

At Christmas and New Year's, she kept the gate open so that anyone could come in and have a meal of rice, meat, and beans. My mom grew vegetables in a garden—cassava, corn, beans. On the holidays, scruffy children would meander into our home, along with homeless people.

A typical kid who did not yet understand the world, I would say things about our odd guests like, "Mom, that man smells."

She would shush me. "It doesn't matter if he smells. He's still a person. A person is a person, no matter what," she said. "You must do what you can to help people. What you do comes back around to you."

It reminded me of the lyrics to a song I had heard in church while growing up: "Goodness returns to you. Wrongdoing also returns to you. Choose which one you want, because it will come back to you." It always scared me. I thought: What if I'm not nice and nothing good happens to me?

I was just beginning to learn about the generosity of our tribe. Eventually I came to understand that there was a spirit of unity among my people, a deeply ingrained sense of helping those less fortunate than you because you could lose your own good fortune at any moment. My people knew that wealth could come and go. My family didn't always have enough food for ourselves for dinner, but we would help anyone who asked. And sometimes, I would be sent to a neighbor's house to ask for help.

"What did you make for dinner?" I would ask the neighbors. And they would send me home with food. We all looked out for one another.

On those nights when we didn't have enough food for dinner, I don't remember feeling upset about it. That's simply the way life was, and I figured it was the same way for everybody. Mom would make a joke and we would laugh it off. She would say something silly or sarcastic, such as, "Tonight we can eat the word of God." Then we would all entertain ourselves by playing cards in the living room. I never felt deprived.

My mother was such a strong, wise, multitasking force. She literally chopped down a tree once while watching Princesse, who was a baby at the time. She situated Princesse over to one side and made sure she chopped the tree so it would fall in the opposite direction. Mom never complained. To this day, I can never complain about anything in front of her. She will say, "Sandra, do you have to chop wood with a child on your back?"

And that pretty much says it all.

FOUR

I STARTED SCHOOL IN KINDERGARTEN, AND I loved it. I was the smart kid, a little nerd. I adored my school uniform and never wanted to take it off. Occasionally I fell asleep in it after school, curled up on the couch. One time when I did this, my brothers and sisters grabbed the opportunity to play a prank on me. I had napped for a few hours, waking up in the evening while it was still light outside. They told me it was the next morning and time to go to school.

"Get up!" they said. "You'll be late for school!"

I hopped up and started getting ready. They were all sitting there, watching me, trying to hold in their laughter. My brother Chris was having an especially hard time keeping a straight face. It occurred to me that they were not getting ready for school themselves.

"What's going on?" I asked. "What's so funny?"

Finally, Princesse said, "Okay, guys, enough." She told me it was early in the evening, not early in the morning. Everyone let loose with their guffaws.

I went to a private school, the best in Uvira. We spoke mostly French and some Swahili, not the language of my people, Kinyamulenge. The different languages were never a problem for me: I had grown up speaking Swahili and knew it well. French came easily to me in school, and I became fluent. My dad would brag to guests that his daughter spoke the best French, and I was so proud. My parents deeply valued education. They had big dreams for their kids, and they knew it all started with school.

"One day, Sandra, you will become president of Congo," Dad used to tell me.

It was important to my dad that both the girls and boys get a good education, which was very forward thinking of him in a community where the traditional role for girls was to marry and produce children. Most families spent all their time and money on the boys. But not my dad. If anything, he stressed the girls' education more. Maybe because he was married to my mom, who was so smart and strong. He really admired her. My parents refused to conform to a lot of things.

For instance, when girls became teenagers in my community, they were often married off. They weren't encouraged to prioritize their education. Sometimes, rival clans would actually try to steal a girl to marry her to their son. A clan once attempted this with my sister Princesse. Boys from the rival clan came and tried to grab her from school, but my brothers fended them off.

It was part of an unfortunate culture, mainly in the villages, in which young men would kidnap a girl, rape her, and then marry her. The rape is committed so that the girl is too ashamed to go back home, or so that her family won't ask for her back. Hundreds, if not thousands, of girls have been married this way. It is one of the reasons why I think my parents were so passionate about educating their girls, so that we could learn that no one can take away our worth.

Another way girls get married in the villages is if a father promises a bride to another father—then their kids grow up and get married. If a man in my family, even one of my brothers, were to promise another man that I would be his bride or his son's bride, I would have to do it. I can't imagine the day my brothers would do such a thing, thanks to my parents, who never gave the boys even the slightest hint that they had any power over the girls.

We were all equals. Even our haircuts were pretty much the same. In school, we had to wear our hair very short, per the rules. It was a sanitary precaution, so that kids wouldn't catch lice from a kid who couldn't bathe every day.

I was ambitious in class. I raised my hand to answer questions and volunteered to go to the chalkboard to solve math problems. But I was also shy with my teachers, afraid to ask them for permission to go to the bathroom. What if they said no? For some reason, the thought of that was intimidating. I kept my head down and studied. I cared deeply about school; I thought if I did the best among my siblings, my parents would love me the most. At home, they were heavily involved in our lessons. During final exams, if we started to fall asleep while studying at night, they would bring a bucket of cold water, put our feet in it, and say, "Keep going!"

Mom made us tea in the mornings, and I walked to school with my brother Alex, carrying a lunch bag and a backpack. The kids at my school all lived within walking distance. That was the only way for any of us to get to school: on our feet. Each morning before classes began, we all lined up in the courtyard by grade, then recited the national anthem and the Lord's Prayer. It was a sweet scene, a courtyard filled with students clad in white and blue.

I was always on time to school. If you arrived late, you

could get a beating. The school had a director of discipline, and he would watch the front gate to see who showed up late. If you were tardy, you would often be told to kneel where you were. Then you would get hit with a stick or ruler—on either your palms or your butt. Sometimes kids could negotiate their punishment: The discipline director would say, "I'll give you ten whacks," and the kids would lobby for five whacks on a hand, five on the rear. Other times, kids who were caught late at the front gate would have to walk to class on their knees. Or they might have to work in the garden, pulling weeds.

You could also get a beating if you didn't know an answer in class, or if you talked out of turn. Discipline was tough. Each class had a designated "chief of class," a student who was in charge of keeping the class in order if the teacher left the room—basically, a spy. We were always nice to the chief of class.

The schools had limited resources, and there were few textbooks. We spent the days learning from our teachers. When I went home, my monkey, Kiki, would be waiting for me by the front gate, jumping up and down. He knew my footsteps and my schedule by heart. I could count on Kiki.

There was always a cloud looming over our school days— the possibility of war. I remember sitting in class and hearing bomb blasts in the distance as rival tribes fought. It was normal to see Congolese soldiers in the streets of Uvira with machine guns. One time, the sound of bombs from some rebellion came close, and the teachers locked us all in the school and told us to take cover under the tables where we did our work. I could feel the ground shaking. I wondered where my parents were, worrying whether they were safe. The school wouldn't let kids leave until their parents came. I waited under the table in fear, until my brother Alex—my sweet little guardian—came and found me. The teachers decided to let us go, even though our parents hadn't arrived yet. We ran through the streets for home. Halfway there, we found our older siblings, who had been out looking for us.

When it came to war, my parents could shelter us from only so much. I knew the sounds of war before I knew how to do a cartwheel. I became accustomed to those sounds. As a kid, I was never afraid of imaginary monsters at night: All the monsters I knew walked in daylight and carried big guns.

One year, when my parents learned from my uncles in the military that my tribe was under threat, we packed up and moved to Burundi. We stayed with a friend of the family named Joyeuse. There were lots of kids at the house, and I became best friends with Shiva, the youngest boy there. All the kids were kind to us, even though they had to share their beds. Shiva was my buddy, but he sounded funny: He spoke Kirundi, a language of Burundi, and I would often ask him to repeat things. Kirundi sounded like a lazy version of Kinyamulenge. Everyone took forever to finish their thoughts in Kirundi. Since I had grown up speaking mostly Swahili, one of the languages of Congo, I was impatient with this slow-sounding language of Burundi. I would interrupt as people were speaking because I couldn't wait for them to finish.

Shiva took me under his wing, just like Alex used to do, and introduced me to some of the neighborhood kids, helping me feel more at home. I began going to school in a hideous uniform: khaki shirt, khaki shorts. I didn't have any friends in my class—Shiva was a couple years ahead of me—and I wanted to get back home. We spoke French in class, but it sounded different from the French I was used to—again, slower. One small thing that brightened my life: Joyeuse bought me a festive little plastic bottle with cartoon characters all over it. I loved it. It had a blue strap so I could sling it over my shoulder, and I filled it with juice or tea and carried it everywhere. And Joyeuse introduced me to a delicious hazelnut-chocolate spread, much like Nutella, that we would slather on bread.

We ended up staying with the family in Burundi for about a year. That was the longest amount of time we were away, but there was rarely a time when our lives weren't inter-rupted in some way by war. Other times, we had to flee to temporary refugee camps.

I was relieved to get home from Burundi and recon-nect with my friends. I resumed my studies, and excelled. My favorite day of school was Proclamation Day. That's the day when our teachers would invite parents to school and announce the rank of the students in each class—from top to bottom—out in the courtyard. It was like our version of a report card, I suppose, only much more public. We would all sit outside and await the results.

For some kids, this was stressful, waiting for their name to be called as the teachers went down the list. No one wanted to be last—it was a monumental embarrassment. For me, the day was fun, because I was confident and always knew I had done well. I consistently made the top three in my class. My dad always said that any of us kids who made the top three could ride home with him in his car. He had a little red Toyota that was so ancient, it was about to die, but I loved that car. It was rare to own a car. I always got to ride home in it from Proclamation Day.

One year, however, I missed a few weeks of school due to a bout of malaria. On Proclamation Day, my teacher called the first name on the list, then the second, then the third.

My name was not among them. My heart pounded. A fourth name was called, and then a fifth. I did not hear my name. I started to cry. Two more names were rattled off. Again, not mine. I thought my chest would burst. Finally, I came in at number eight. I was heartbroken. I wanted to be a star. My parents tried to comfort me.

"Remember, you missed a lot of classes because you were sick," Mom said, putting her arm around me, trying to console me.

Dad said I could ride in the car because he was proud that I had done well despite the malaria. I refused to ride in the car; I didn't deserve it. My siblings tried to tell me that it was okay, that I was still brilliant. Alex even offered to give up his seat for me.

Alex, who was a year ahead of me in school, had a Proclamation Day where he didn't do so well either. In fact, he did so poorly, he had to repeat the fifth grade. That year, we went to fifth grade together. He was none too pleased about that, especially when I couldn't resist teasing him. But he was such a sport. I knew he always had my back.

Around this time, I set my sights on becoming a television journalist. The reporters on TV dazzled me, and I wanted to be just like them. I would practice at home, putting on nightly news broadcasts for my family, speaking in French. I loved showing off to my dad especially, since he also spoke French very well. For my broadcasts, I interviewed my mom about what she cooked for dinner, questioned my dad about work, and did investigations about the origins of various household items. I could tell that my parents were proud of me.

At school, the Congolese kids were not always so supportive. They would tease me, mainly because my nose was thinner than theirs, making me look different. Sometimes they would say I wasn't truly Congolese. Other times they would call me Rwandan. It was meant to be an insult, making me into a foreigner, but I didn't know what it meant.

"I'm not Rwandan," I would say. "I've never been to Rwanda. I was born here."

I didn't understand. I didn't know anything about Rwanda, besides being able to point to it on a map. The kids who targeted me probably didn't understand what they were accusing me of either. They were repeating what they heard from their parents. I would tell Alex when other kids taunted me, and he would get into fights with them. My parents told us to ignore slurs.

They were determined to raise us peacefully, even though we were growing up in a conflict zone. They taught us tolerance and forgiveness. I didn't understand why the Congolese kids were mean to us. I wanted to say to them, "Don't you have parents who teach you respect?" When I complained to my parents, they said not to take the jabs from the other kids to heart. They always helped me keep perspective.

"Did they injure you in some way?" Mom would ask. "Do you have a wound?"

FIVE

that I will never forget: the day my mother locked herself in her bedroom and would not come out. I had never seen her disappear like that, and I didn't understand what was wrong. Then my sister Princesse took me aside and explained: My favorite uncle, Rumenge, the officer who always brought me treats and new clothes, had been killed in one of the conflicts in the region.

"Mom's heart is broken," Princesse said.

When my mother finally emerged from her room the next day, it was as if all the joy had been drained from her body. She loved Rumenge deeply. There is an old photograph of Rumenge with Deborah and me, the only picture I have of him, or of Deborah. It's also the only photo of my face from before the massacre. I don't know my own face from back then. All of our family albums burned in the fiery attack. A friend of the family found this single remaining photo and sent it to us years after the tragedy—a little postcard from another world.

My mother was so sad when she lost Rumenge, she had no appetite. She became thin, and looked like a different person. She woke up every day worrying about frightening things that could happen to her other relatives. She spent her nights and days crying. She couldn't focus. She seemed so far away from the rest of us, in her own world. My uncle had left some clothes at the house, and she took them out and sat with them for days. Princesse took over for her and ran the family, which was one of the many reasons I looked up to her.

Before my uncle died, he gave my mom a hundred dollars, which was a great deal of money at the time. But Mom didn't want to buy anything with it because it was the last thing he had given her. She wanted to save it forever. A friend suggested that she use the money to start a small business, which would help the family and also keep her busy, so she could try to get past her grief. Mom gave it some thought and eventually decided to indeed use the money to help her family, which Rumenge would have liked.

And so, one day, she bought a refrigerator and started a little café in our home. She kept things like soft drinks and milk in the fridge, and sold them along with snacks. People started coming by regularly, sipping a drink, chatting. Our house got even busier. Later, she started trading cows. My mom was the original feminist. Selling cows and running businesses were considered jobs for men, but she did her own thing. She was a true trailblazer.

She once told me that around this time a song came to her in a dream. She loved writing and singing songs, but she had been so filled with sadness that she had lost the heart to sing. Then the lyrics came to her in bed one night: "You are not to spend your days worrying about tomorrow." The song helped give her strength. She no longer woke up worrying about her relatives and what might happen to them. She focused instead on her new business—on inventory and profits—to help us all move ahead in life.

On the balmy evenings in our little café, we would play popular music on the radio, and Alex and I would dance for the customers. We loved dancing. It was one of our favorite forms of entertainment. We didn't have laptops or cell phones like kids in America have today. We didn't have birthday parties with gobs of goodie bags. We didn't get stacks of presents to unwrap at Christmas. But we didn't need a lot of material things to amuse ourselves. We had something better: dancing. We would dance and vigorously shake our butts and hips—twerking, basically. Where I come from, twerking is not sexualized the way it is in America. The boys sometimes do it better than the girls. Everyone does it. It's wild and fun and freeing, not about sex.

As my mom found her footing, my dad seemed to struggle: He was often stressed and distracted, as my missing brother, Heritage, was always on his mind. Dad was frequently away from home, either trying to find Heritage or working. Sometimes he missed events in my life, like Proclamation Day, but our house was always so crowded with friends and relatives, I didn't really notice. My father tried everything to locate Heritage and bring him home. He offered to buy his son back from the military with cows; he offered to take his son's place, to no avail.

Dad was very protective of all his kids. He knew my brothers Chris and Alex could be kidnapped by the military, just like Heritage. And girls could be grabbed and raped. Rape is a serious weapon of war in Congo. Tens of thousands of women have been raped in civil war over the years.

There were United Nations peacekeepers in our region,

but they did not really make me feel safe. They flirted inappropriately with my older sisters' friends. One of the peacekeepers became romantically involved with one of Adele's friends: He would take the girl out drinking, then take her back to the UN compound. He was a grown man, taking advantage of a teen girl. Growing up, the only white men I ever saw worked for either the UN or UNICEF. They wore uniforms and drove around in trucks and looked important. You wouldn't approach them or try to talk to them. I equated white men with power and authority and thought America must be full of white men.

In 2002, when I was around eight years old, my father heard some heart-stopping news from a friend: Heritage had been spotted in the Congolese city of Bukavu, beaten up and brutalized. My dad went to find him and bring him home. Turned out, Heritage was in such bad shape that he was no longer of any use to the army, and the soldiers released him from their grip. He could have easily disappeared and died there. The army didn't want to pay for a child soldier's medical care.

When Heritage came home, he was in his teens, and he knew nothing but violence. When I saw him for the first time, he looked like a monster with a bloody face, a swollen eye. That is my first memory of my brother. I could barely bring myself to look at him and his scary eye. My mom and dad took him to get medical treatment, and he emerged all wrapped up in bandages like a mummy. Then my parents tucked him away in a bedroom in our home. They kept it very dark in there because the light hurt his eye. Sometimes I would peer into his room out of curiosity, but I was afraid of him.

Over time, as he began to recuperate physically, I grew to know him a little better. I learned that the soldiers who kidnapped him gave the kids guns and made them shoot people to prove they were good fighters. The military got the kids hooked on weed and alcohol to make them more compliant. Heritage had temper issues from his traumatic ordeal. After a few months at home, he went to live with a friend of the family in Burundi. My parents wanted to hide him away there. They didn't want to take a chance that the army would come and snatch him again.

SIX

WAR WASN'T THE ONLY SOURCE OF TROUBLE in our lives. In the rainy season, the river would rise up and flood the streets, and we would have to leave home in a hurry. For some reason, the floods always happened in the middle of the night. We would hear the rushing roar of water coming, and my dad would lock up the house and get us all out of there to head for higher ground. Kiki would climb to safety at the top of the front gate. My first memory of being afraid in life was during one of those floods: I remember holding hands with one of my uncles and running as fast as I could uphill to escape the rising water. I ran so fast, it felt like my feet didn't touch the ground.

My mom would soothe us. She was always a calming presence. In fact, she wrote a song for each of us kids with lyrics predicting a happy fate. My song says, "In all that God has made, you're the most beautiful of all." In my language, it sounds like this: "Muby'Imana yaremye byose, ntakindi cyiza kukurusha."

I was born with dark skin, but in my culture, light skin is considered a sign of beauty, so Mom wrote in my song that I would become fairer skinned. In fact, I did. It embarrasses me to think that skin color should have anything to do with supposed beauty, but that is the culture. For a time, my nickname became "Mazobe," a term for fair skin.

For my brother Alex, who was born small, my mom spun a song that he was kindhearted and genuine and would grow up to become strapping and tall. And indeed, he did grow into a handsome, muscular young man. For my sister Deborah, Mom wrote that she was so beautiful, she would get at least one hundred cows when she wed. The song said that anyone with ninety-nine cows needn't bother. I'm sure that prediction would have come true too.

In addition to the creative songs Mom wrote, she had an inherent sense of style, and she bought me the snazziest outfits. Sometimes she would pick fabrics of bright colors and patterns and take them to the tailor to have traditional cotton dresses made for me. Congo has some of the best, most fashionable tailors in the world. Other times she would buy outfits from more Western-style stores. For every major holiday—Christmas, Easter—I would get a new outfit for church. It was always an exciting day to get new clothes and new shoes for the holidays.

One year for Christmas, Mom bought me one of my favorite outfits—a pink polka-dot skirt and top with a matching collar. She bought Deborah the same outfit in blue. My brother Chris took us on a walk around the neighborhood, so we could show off our new clothes. We ended up coming home with two kids from the neighborhood, and they joined us for Christmas dinner. Once again, our doors were open.

My family was Christian, and we went to church every Sunday. The service lasted all day long and involved lots of singing and clapping. Church was a major part of our community. Our people were close-knit, and everyone knew everyone's business: If you ever skipped services on a Sunday, people would ask, "Why weren't you in church?"

Another big part of our community—and a personal favorite of mine—was an elaborate dance procession performed by the neighborhood kids. It was a glamorous reenactment of a wedding, with a "bride and groom" surrounded by dancing girls and drumming boys. The boys made the drums from empty tin cans of Nido, a powdered milk drink made by Nestlé. To create the drums, the boys stretched thick plastic bags tightly across the tops of the cans, securing the bags with rubber bands. They used different sizes of cans, with each size creating a unique sound. The kids in the neighborhood all knew one another, and they raised money for the event, which was held several times a year. At the end of each performance, they hosted a reception, serving rice and beans, and Fanta and Coke in glass bottles.

I couldn't wait to be old enough to participate. The kids would spend weeks choreographing the event and making up songs, and I would attend the rehearsals, dreaming of a day when I could be a dancer in the procession. I watched my sister Adele and her fabulous friends, wanting to be like them. On the day of the event, the kids—twelve dancing girls and eight drumming boys—would march and twirl through the streets of the neighborhood, around twenty blocks in all, while families lined up to watch. The bride and groom would walk along at the center of the procession, with six girls in front and six in back, and rows of boys on each side. The girls wore black T-shirts and bright, short wrap skirts to accentuate their butts, with spandex shorts underneath, stretchy and flexible for twerking. It was always sunny and hot, and everyone worked up a sweat. It was like a big moving concert.

No one really knows how the tradition got started, but different neighborhoods each had their own processions. It was a way for kids to entertain themselves.

Finally, when I was ten years old, I got to take part in the fun. The kids made me the bride, which was embarrassing because that meant I would be paired with a boy as my groom. At that point in my life, I thought, Ewww, boys! My brothers and sisters teased me during the practice sessions, where I sat with my groom, a boy named Merewe, while the dancing girls learned their routines. I didn't want to be the bride; I wanted to dance. My brothers made my life a living nightmare with their taunting.

"Sandra, you might end up marrying that boy one day!" Alex said.

I worried that if he kept saying it, it might turn out to be true. However, on the upside, my mom bought me a beautiful light-blue dress to wear for the performance. It was silky and puffy, like a dress for a princess, with a sash that tied in the back.

On the day of the performance, my dad drove me to the starting point of the procession in his car, and my groom, Merewe, came to take my hand. I was embarrassed and also laughing so hard, I was about to cry. Merewe was nervous too. I didn't talk to him at all. In fact I barely looked at him.

I didn't want anyone to think I liked him. As we began our slow march through the neighborhood streets, I felt jittery about being the center of attention, but also kind of thrilled. My groom and I walked side by side, silently—our job was to look cute. I could feel everyone's eyes on me. I wanted to impress our audience, and the older girls who danced.

That was in April 2004, around Easter time. It would be my first and last procession. I never got to be a dancer because a couple months later, we would be fleeing Uvira.

Most of the girls who danced around me that day later died in the massacre.

SEVEN

IN JUNE 2004, THE TENSIONS TOWARD MY people escalated quickly. The Congolese kids at school were calling me Rwandan all the time, dubbing me a foreigner, repeating what they had heard at home.

"You're Rwandan!" they would yell.

I would give them my standard reply. "I'm not. I've never been there."

Some teachers were even warning us during class, implying that trouble was coming. My parents heard rumors at work. My father tried hard to shelter us, but he couldn't control what we heard at school or on the street. All signs pointed to another interrupted year.

I was busy getting ready for school one morning when Dad left and returned home in a yellow minivan, with a stranger at the wheel. Dad came hurrying into the house, a worried look on his face. He was wearing black dress pants and a black shirt and looked as if he might be going somewhere special, perhaps for work. Then again, he was always dressed up, so I wasn't sure if anything was wrong or not. I had finished getting dressed for school, and was preparing to head out with Alex. Chris and Adele had already left for their school, which was a few miles away. Princesse was at home with us; she was a senior that year and had been preparing for the national exam to earn her diploma.

My dad told us to wait and not go anywhere. He went into a bedroom with my mom and they talked in hushed whispers. Then they walked out together.

"Sandra, you need to pack," Dad said.

We would be leaving home again.

I went to my room and took off my school uniform so I wouldn't soil it on our trip. Then I pulled out a big copper-colored suitcase with buckles that locked on top. The first thing I packed was my pale-blue dress from the dance procession. It was the most useless thing to take to a refugee camp, of course. And I knew I probably wouldn't wear it, but still, I wanted it with me. In fact, I wanted all of my fanciest clothes with me, so I packed my church clothes. I was ten years old, and it was the first time I was really old enough to pack for myself. I was quite proud of my packing decisions. I helped Deborah pack too, and she also wanted her prettiest, most impractical outfits.

My parents had no time to supervise our efforts. They said we needed to leave immediately. My dad asked our neighbors—who were not members of our tribe and did not need to flee—to get an urgent message to Chris and Adele to leave school and head for the mountains to stay with our grandparents. We all figured it was just another temporary exodus. We had to leave my pet monkey, Kiki, behind, but I assumed I would be back soon.

Thus we began the journey that is forever seared in my mind. We crammed into the yellow van. I sat by the window in the second row, with Deborah, Princesse, and Heritage next to me. Heritage had recently returned home from Burundi, looking much healthier.

Mom sat with two neighbors in the back. Dad sat up front with the driver. Weaving through the streets of Uvira, we watched people frantically trying to get out of the city. Desperate people knocked on our vehicle when we slowed down, begging to get inside.

"I'm sorry, there's no space," my father called to them.

I sat there, dazed, thinking we might be away from home longer than usual this time.

We drove for about forty-five minutes, with Dad discussing different routes with Mom and the driver. Then suddenly we were stopped at a checkpoint, or rather, an ambush. A blockade of chairs, benches, and tables lay across the road, and men stood there with guns, forcing us to stop. On the side of the road, a mob of angry Congolese people stood— men, women, and children. They wore mostly civilian clothes, although some had military-style pants. They carried machetes, knives, and rifles.

The crowd rushed toward us and began shaking the minivan. We braced ourselves. It felt as if the van might tip over. We had mattresses and suitcases tied to the top of the vehicle, and the attackers tore them down and stole them. We hurried to lock the doors and tried to close the windows, but the windows were stuck open—the vehicle was rusty and old, ready to fall apart. People reached in, grabbing at us. They ripped our watches off our wrists. I had always known that many Congolese people disliked us, but I had never seen such hate on people's faces.

Even little kids were shaking the van angrily. Why are these kids so furious? I thought. They don't even know us. I didn't understand what was happening. I thought children were supposed to respect their elders, but they were throwing rocks and sand at all of us, my parents included. We tried to dodge the rocks flying at our heads. Some of the kids had guns. People were spitting at us. Deborah and I were crying, and my parents looked defenseless.

Then the driver got out of the van, took the keys, and walked away, leaving us there to be attacked. He was Congolese, and I think he drove us there on purpose. I wondered how we could ever escape. Princesse put her arms around Deborah and me, holding us close.

Amid the chaos, a grown man—he appeared to be in his forties—marched up to the van, looking like he wanted to kill us. He reached in through the window and punched Deborah in the face. Completely shocked and in pain, she began wailing. I couldn't fathom it. Why would a man punch a six-year-old child in the face? I cried hysterically too, and Princesse tried to calm us down. I wondered what Deborah was thinking. She was probably wondering: Why aren't my mom and dad protecting me? My parents were helpless. They were trying to calm Heritage, who was having a breakdown— no doubt the result of post-traumatic stress from his time as a child soldier. He wanted to get out of the van and fight with people. My parents were trying to keep him inside.

Then one of our neighbors in the back of the van started

shouting, "I'm not a soldier! I'm not a soldier!" I wondered why he was saying that. Perhaps he feared that we were under attack because the Congolese thought we were some kind of rebels, although we certainly didn't look the part.

We were completely exposed, with no way out. We must have sat there for almost an hour, waiting to die. We couldn't jump out into the mob. But we couldn't move the car without keys. It was the longest hour of my life. We so easily could have all been killed right there. But then, a miracle: an angel appeared. A young Congolese man wearing a striped polo shirt and sporting a cool haircut pushed his way through the crowd to the van. He looked like Will Smith when he starred in *The Fresh Prince of Bel-Air*.

"Why are you still here?" he asked us.

"Our driver left with the keys," Dad said. "We can't move."

"You need to get out of here," the man said. "Or you are going to die."

The man asked what our driver looked like, and my dad described him. Then the man left and, remarkably, returned ten minutes later, forcing his way through the mob again. He had the keys. He managed to wedge himself into the car. People didn't try to fight him since he was Congolese.

"I'm going to drive out of here as fast as possible," he said. "We'll see what happens."

This good-hearted stranger saved our lives. I will never forget him. There was nothing in it for him to help us—in fact, he could have been killed for doing so—but he sped toward the blockade of furniture, finding a weak spot on one side where there were just a few chairs piled on top of one another. He smashed through the chairs, crunching them beneath the wheels, and got us out of there. People were going crazy, running after the van. We were all crying and screaming. I heard gunfire and kept my head down.

This mysterious man drove us to the Congolese border, which was jammed with crowds of people trying to get out of the country and head into Burundi. We piled out of the van. None of us had really processed the attack. We were too shaken up. Our suitcases inside the van had not been stolen, and we yanked them out. Dad thanked our driver, this mystical being. The young man drove off, and I hope and pray that he survived after saving our lives.

I will never know. At the border, we climbed into a giant semitruck run by the refugee arm of the United Nations, the UNHCR. The truck was built to carry cargo, not people, and it was smelly and disgusting, packed full of bodies. It reeked like rotten food. We were jammed in there so tightly, we could barely move. Everyone was hot and sweaty, the kind of sweat that smells like fear. The back door of the truck was left open so we could breathe, but people had to hang on for their lives and be careful not to tumble out onto the road. We drove for about a half hour into Burundi, and then stopped at an empty field near a town called Gatumba. The sun was starting to set.

That empty field was our home for the night.

EIGHT

THE FIRST NIGHT IN THE FIELD, WE ALL SLEPT outside on the ground, a bunch of displaced, frazzled families, uncertain of what was to come. There were hundreds of us. We had no tents or mattresses, and no food. My dad went out foraging and returned with a handful of snacks he bought from kids selling them by the side of the road—peanuts and mandazi, little round cakes. The field stretched along a highway that ran from Burundi to Congo, and cars whizzed by us as we lay in the dirt. The land smelled of fertilizer and livestock from a nearby farm. The ground was hard and damp, and mosquitoes feasted on us. The evening air was cooler than we were accustomed to, and officials from the UNHCR handed out itchy dark-gray blankets. Those blankets were so scratchy, I wondered if the person who designed them thought: How can I make the world's worst blanket? No one slept much that night.

The next morning, the UNHCR officials started building tents. They put some strong logs in the ground and stretched green tarps across the top. Our new homes. The tents were separated into "rooms," with sheets of tarp serving as "walls," but there was no privacy. There were women's tents and men's tents. We had nothing, no furniture, no mosquito nets, just thin mattresses placed flat on the ground. It took several days for officials to deliver food. In the meantime, Dad bought snacks from the kids by the roadside. My parents said the situation was temporary, and I think they really believed that. We had been displaced before. I thought we would just have to endure this incredibly uncomfortable camp for a little while.

Life in a refugee camp is bizarre: There's no school, nothing to do. No toys for kids, no dolls, no distractions. People sit there all day long. For the first week, I thought it was kind of exciting because some of my friends were there; their families had fled the city like us, grabbing rides however they could. Since my friends were now living within a few feet of me, we could hang out all day and eat dinner with my parents at night, kind of like an endless slumber party.

My friends called my parents "Mama Sandra" and "Papa Sandra." We didn't use terms like "Mr." and "Mrs." In my culture, that would be considered impersonal and disrespectful. I loved eating meals with my friends every night. My best friends were there, two girls around my age named Justine and Ziraje, and a boy named Inge. We would hang out together during the day, looking for things to do, thinking up games to entertain ourselves. We played one game with a ball made of wadded-up plastic bags and rubber bands: One of us would stand in the middle of two others, and we would try to hit the person in the middle with the ball, sort of like dodgeball.

Sometimes, young men from Burundi would come to the camp with bikes to see if anyone wanted to be taken anywhere, and my brother Alex managed to befriend some of them. This was a huge bonus, because they would let us play with their bikes. Alex taught me tricks on the bike, like how to let go of the handlebars while I rode.

Weeks went by. I missed school terribly. But I continued to think that we would be going home.

My siblings and I spent much of our time in line for water, standing with empty jugs to fill from a giant plastic tank in a blue tent. The water tank was huge, the size of a spacious living room. Trucks would come regularly and pump water into the tank. The line for water was always crowded, and sometimes the water would run out after we waited in line all day. We went there almost every day. I was so little that I would often get pushed to the back of the line. I was never successful in retrieving water from that tank. My older siblings were much better at it.

For food, each family had a card to show the authorities to get their rations. Every few weeks, UN workers would deliver the rations of rice, beans, vegetable oil, sugar, salt, and a flour mixture called sosoma, made of soybeans, sorghum, and corn. The amount of food you got depended on the number of people in your family. There was no variation in our meals—no greens, no meat, no fish. The women cooked with clay stoves fueled by coal, and the camp always smelled of fire and smoke. People were provided with pots for cooking, but some women had brought their own. Many of my family's things had been stolen on the drive to the camp, but we still had our photo albums, which my mom had grabbed on the way out of the house. I would often flip through them with my friends since we had so little to do.

On the days the food was delivered, I got depressed. It was as if we had been reduced to beggars. Mom and Dad waited in line with their card for their designated food supply, and it was disheartening to see my parents so powerless.

All of us kids in the camp could see that our parents were no longer in control. How could parents assure their kids that everything would be fine when we could see how vulnerable they were? They couldn't hide it. We appreciated the food, but it was a demeaning and demoralizing experience.

The camp had a handful of outhouses, separated for women and men. The toilet consisted of a hole in the ground, unsanitary and smelly. To bathe, we put water in a bucket and splashed ourselves with it, using soap we bought from local vendors via the kids on bikes. It was a far cry from our comfy house back in Uvira with indoor plumbing.

Every day I dreamed of going home. I couldn't fully comprehend why we had been displaced, why people would resent us so much that they would drive us from our homes into this barren, desolate place.

We tried our best to stay positive. At six o'clock in the morning every day, people would gather outside in the middle of the camp for prayers with the pastor. Sometimes I would go with Deborah and my mom; other times I would sleep in, waking to people singing and clapping—happy sounds. Every Sunday, people gathered for church in the courtyard. On the cool, crisp mornings, I would nestle with Mom, resting my head on her shoulder.

At one point, some of us kids were taken to the Congolese

embassy in the capital of Burundi to take final exams. Congo had national finals for sixth and twelfth grades. I was in sixth grade, and I went. We were offered food at the embassy, but I was too nervous to eat. The kids who did eat—including Princesse, who was in twelfth grade—got very sick, throwing up from food poisoning. The Congolese workers at the embassy had tampered with the food. Even the schoolkids were targets. I never got the results of my exam.

We returned to the refugee camp and continued to sit there in the heat with nothing to do, day after day. And then came that fateful night, when the sound of gunfire approached while Deborah and I lay down to sleep. I never imagined it would be the last night I would see my little sister alive.

NINE

THE KILLERS WHO ATTACKED OUR CAMP WERE
rebels from Burundi, and they did not want us there. We
were outsiders again. On that night, I thought my life was
over. My mother and sister had been gunned down. I had
blacked out from fear, then tried to flee, only to find a gun
pointed at my head. I don't know why the gunman didn't
shoot me on the spot. Perhaps he didn't want to waste a
precious bullet on a little girl. I was just a girl, after all, so
how could I possibly survive? I imagine this is what he was
thinking.

In that moment, with the gun to my head, people rushed
all around us in a fiery blur—shooting, fleeing, screaming.

It must have been just a second or two that I stood there, expecting to die, but it felt like an eternity. The man, the gun, and me, in my red shorts and khaki tank top, frozen in time. I closed my eyes. No way out. There was no time to think anyway. I suppose, in that instant, I felt more peace than panic. It was all beyond my control.

Then, in a flash amid the chaos, somehow I got kicked to the ground. The gunman went chasing after someone else. Fate had given me another chance. I got up and fled. I stumbled, I fell, I ran. Around me people were burning, crying in pain, dying. Those who still had legs were scrambling in all directions, running for their lives. I tumbled into a ditch that served as a garbage dump for the camp. I waded through the trash and sludge, and kept moving forward. I had no idea where I was going. I just ran.

I made it to the fields of a nearby farm. I could hear people talking in the dark. I went to hide behind a tree, but I was not alone. A woman was there, and I tensed up. I didn't know if she was one of my people.

"Where are your parents?" she asked me. She was one of us.

"I think my mom is dead," I said.

She took me by the hand and we wandered through the bumpy fields in the dark, passing the haunted faces of survivors. I spotted an uncle, Ezekiel, and he said to me, "Why aren't you with your mother?"

"I think she died," I said.

"No," he said. "I saw her. She's not dead."

"But I saw her die," I said, confused. "She was shot."

"No, no," he said. "She is alive."

I didn't know what to think. I couldn't tell what was real. Ezekiel joined us and we searched for my mother, tapping women on the shoulder as they sat, hunched over, on the ground, or stood in stunned silence. I desperately wanted Mom to be alive. I prayed that Ezekiel was right. The thought of continuing my life without my mother was too much to bear. She was my strength, my inspiration. With her, I felt safe and loved. Who would take care of me if she died?

"I'm not her," each woman said, turning to look at me with vacant eyes.

"I'm not her."

"I'm not her."

We kept tapping women on the shoulder. I thought Ezekiel must have been mistaken. Perhaps he had simply seen someone who looked like my mother. Why was he insisting that she was alive, taking me on this search and breaking my heart all over again?

And then, like an image from a dream, Mom appeared

before me. She was standing by herself, wrapped in a sheet, and very alone. She looked as if her world had ended. I had never seen my mom look like that, not even when my uncle Rumenge had died years earlier. I couldn't believe it was her.

"Is that you?" she asked me, studying my face, as if she couldn't believe I was real either.

We hugged each other hard, but I couldn't trust my eyes, or my arms. Was it really her? I kept feeling her, touching her body, her hands, her arms, up and down, again and again. I hit her on the arm to make sure she was not an apparition.

"I'm fine," she said. "Don't worry."

But she was not fine. I could see a gaping hole in her side from the gunfire. She was bleeding, shivering in pain. I held on to her, clinging to her gently but firmly at the same time.

"Are you hurt?" she asked me.

And then a realization swept through my body as if I had been torn apart by bullets myself: My mother was not with Deborah. My little sister had been clinging to my mom during the attack, never leaving her side. The last time I saw Deborah, she was holding tight to my mother's side. And then there were the sparks of gunfire. I looked Mom in the eyes, searching, and she looked back. She knew what I was thinking. And I could see the truth in her eyes. I sobbed. I couldn't imagine the world without Deborah in it, my beautiful little sister, my soulful young friend who thought I could do no wrong.

Deborah died in the clothes she wore to bed that night, including my hand-me-down soccer jersey that she loved. The jersey had always been my favorite—a blue Brazil jersey, with the number 9 on the back. When it was mine, I made my mom wash it constantly so I could wear it as much as possible. It had become Deborah's favorite too. Now she would never wear my clothes again. She would not grow up with me.

"I'm sorry," my mother said, holding me close. "I'm so sorry."

She told me they were all gone—Deborah, my aunt, my two young cousins who had held Mom's hands as they marched from the tent to their death, lured by the men who promised to help them. She thought I had been killed too. Mom had been left for dead in a pile of bleeding bodies. Deborah had been shot in the head, but she survived long enough to say the heartbreaking words to my mom, "Hold me."

My mother managed to hold Deborah on her chest as my little sister died, something a mother should never have to do. Mom, covered in blood, heard the attackers talk about torching the pile of bodies she lay in, and she managed to remove the bodies on top of her and quietly crawl away. She decided she would rather be shot dead trying to escape than be burned alive. But my brave and resilient mom did escape. She headed for the farm, following other people who were fleeing, and falling into the same garbage ditch that I did along the way.

Mom did not know if my father or Alex had survived. She thought not. But she said she had seen Heritage and then lost sight of him.

And so we set out to find Heritage together, weaving through the lost souls in the night. Exhausted and overwhelmed, we didn't say much to each other. I tried to keep my thoughts focused on finding Heritage, not to think about Dad and Alex, since we knew nothing of their fate. I could not bear to think about what might have happened to them. Just hours ago, we had all been drifting off to sleep, and now our lives, our families, our people, were torn apart.

As we scoured the farm, people were weeping for lost children, whimpering in pain, or sitting silently, staring at nothing. The air smelled of dewy grass, damp soil, sweat, and death. Dawn was coming soon. People who lived in cozy homes on the outskirts of the farm were waking up, turning on their lights, unaware of the bloody massacre that had taken place across the fields that night, turning our camp into a fiery hell. At that point, there were no policemen, no officials, no one to help us, just my butchered tribe.

I wondered if I would ever see my father and Alex again.

TEN

IT MUST HAVE BEEN AROUND FIVE O'CLOCK in the morning when we found Heritage. His arms were practically falling off his body from gunshot wounds, but he was acting like he was just fine. So stoic, so brave, my brother. He knew violence all too well.

My mother and I embraced him, trying not to hurt him with our grip. I asked the question I was afraid to hear him answer: "Have you seen Dad and Alex?" They had been living in the same tent with Heritage. I braced myself for his reply.

"Yes," he said. "They are alive."

My heart flooded with relief. I would get to see them,

hug them, again. Heritage had spotted them amid the chaos and confusion but had lost them. And so we set out once again, searching the ghostly faces.

It was light out when we found them, the sun rising slowly in a pale-blue sky, casting a warm glow over the fields of sorrow and grief. I remember thinking: How dare the sun rise, as if it were any other day, after such a gruesome night.

People all around us were weeping so loudly, it sounded like a choir. A chorus of tears.

Oddly, Alex was wearing a sparkly red shirt designed for girls and a too-small pair of shorts for girls too.

"What are you wearing?" I asked him. "Where did you get those clothes?"

He explained that he had been sleeping in the nude when the killers attacked his tent, and he took off running, naked.

"No time to get dressed!" he said. When he reached the farm fields, he said, a family from a nearby home brought him the clothes to cover his body.

My dad stood by his side, strong and tall. He had holes in the collar of his shirt from bullets. Even his belt strap had bullet holes, but no bullets had brought him down. I stared at the holes in his shirt collar, amazed. We all hugged again and again, holding one another tight. But the reunion felt strangely awkward too. We did not mention Deborah. I think everyone sensed that she was no longer with us, but no one could bear to say that she was gone. Dad looked like he was trying to hold himself together. Our lives would never be the same. Our Deborah was gone. Our dreams would forever be haunted by her memory. But for now, we had each other.

Alex was telling me a rush of stories. "A bullet just missed my eye!" he said.

He described how a woman had been cooking in his tent when the killers came. While trying to escape, she stepped into the pot of scalding-hot beans. Confused by the burning pain, she screamed, "I've been shot!" Alex called out to her, "No, you haven't! Take your foot out of those beans!" Just one more insane image from our night of hell.

Officials from Burundi and the UN were finally arriving now. Buses were coming to bring people to the hospital. Mom refused to go to the hospital, despite the gunshot wound in her side. She said she would go later. For the time being, she wanted to stay with our family. And I'm sure she did not want to leave Deborah behind. We all stuck together, tired and broken.

I found my cousin Inge. He had survived, but he had lost his mother and two little brothers. I don't know how he could handle losing so many family members in one night. I remember feeling that I wasn't entitled to cry because others had lost even more than I had. I learned that my friend Ziraje had been killed. I would never see her face again. My friend Justine survived, and I saw her briefly, but we got separated and it would be the last time I ever saw her. Two of my closest childhood friends, gone from my life in a night.

Inge and I sat together with his brother Desire that morning beside a fence near a highway, looking out over the eerie scene. For a long time, we didn't talk. We just stared in disbelief. Devastated people were scattered across the fields, our friends, neighbors, and relatives, facing unthinkable grief. Mothers were screaming and wailing at the thought of leaving their children's bodies behind. I saw a baby with full-body burns. Children were wandering aimlessly, staring blankly, not yet old enough to grasp what had happened. Some had lost both of their parents. I had never seen people look so desperate. Mothers were lifeless. Their entire lives had been taken from them. None of us kids could understand what was going on.

I had a sense of shock and confusion, jumbled emotions. We had seen the horror, but we couldn't understand it. We were so young, so confused, that Inge and I did what kids do: We teased Alex about the girls' clothes he was wearing. "Nice outfit," I said.

I asked my mom if Inge and Desire would live with

us now since they had nowhere to go. But my family had nowhere to live either.

We all walked across the charred remains of the camp, wading through a sea of crumpled bodies and limbs. I could not comprehend that you could spend time with people one day and then pick up their body parts the next. We looked for the remains of Deborah, my cousins, and my aunt. We found Deborah near where our tent had been.

"That's her skull," Mom said.

It was the most horrifying scene imaginable. Somehow my mom found the strength to cradle my little sister's burned skull in her arms. We saw the row of people who had been shot dead while running from the tent when the attack began. We found my cousin's body, which had not been burned.

I didn't understand death yet. I knew that older people died, and I knew that people could get sick and die, but not kids. I had never thought about how children could die, especially such a violent death. I thought someone would come and say it was all a dream. I wanted to wake up from this nightmare.

We saw officials stuffing people's limbs into long white plastic body bags, just picking up different people's limbs and throwing them into the bags. I stared; I didn't cry. It was too much to absorb. You're not supposed to see the limbs of your friends and relatives crammed into plastic bags, all tangled up together because no one knows who the limbs belong to.

At the time, we didn't know who had come to kill us. We learned later that a brutal militia group from Burundi had carried out the attack: Forces Nationales de Libération, led by a man named Agathon Rwasa. The group claimed responsibility through a spokesman, Pasteur Habimana. Members of other militia groups were reportedly involved in the attack as well, including one called Interahamwe. Of the some 800 refugees in the camp, 166 were reportedly killed and 116 injured. The killers were not brought to justice.

But all we knew on that morning was that we had nowhere to go. We had no home. We had nothing, not even the suitcases we had brought with us to the refugee camp. We didn't even have our family photos. Mom's albums had gone up in flames with everything else in the tent.

It had been more than thirty hours since I had slept. I don't recall the rest of the day, or the night. Everything became a blur. I remember seeing the body bags. I remember thinking: How will we stay alive?

And I remember a feeling of disbelief that Deborah had been taken from me. When you lose someone, you're supposed to have time to say good-bye, time to cry, time to mourn. We never got to bury Deborah. I never saw her grave. I didn't even get to see her face after she died. If only I had known that I would never see her again, I would have spent the years learning every curve on her face, studying those long eyelashes, memorizing the way her lips curled into a funny little twist when she was happy. I would have paid more attention. When I think of her infectious smile and those black curls and big dark eyes, I can't help but wonder what my baby sister would look like now. She would be eighteen years old today if her life hadn't been cut short. Beauty like that was never meant to last in this cruel world.

Sometimes I have a terrifying thought: What if I forget Deborah's face? The years take me further and further from her. I meet people who never knew she existed. I feel as if the older I get, the more I am losing her. As a child, my future always had Deborah in it. The memories haunt me: One second I am there beside her, falling asleep, and the next, I am watching her die. I never got to say good-bye.

ELEVEN

I WOKE UP IN THE HOME OF A RELATIVE NEAR the capital of Burundi. I don't remember how I got there. I was like a zombie. There were six kids in that family. We called their dad, Mutware, our uncle. His mom and my father's mom are related. In our culture, they would be considered brothers. Some of my cousins there were around my age, and I could tell they didn't know how to wrap their heads around what had happened to us. They had no idea how to play with me or how to cheer me up. The house was tiny, and my traumatized family had suddenly piled in there with nowhere else to go. Everyone seemed confused.

Heritage, Alex, and Mom had all checked into the hospital.

Heritage was in critical condition with bullets in both arms. Alex had a bullet fragment in his eye. Mom had the devastating gunshot wound in her abdomen. It was remarkable that they were still alive. My sister Princesse—who had been away at the choir concert on the night of the attack—reunited with them in the hospital. I went to visit everyone there, and was horrified by what I saw. The hospital was vastly overcrowded. Some of the survivors were helping clean wounds and change dressings for others. There weren't enough people on staff to handle the influx of broken bodies.

Heritage's wounds to his arms were so ghastly, I couldn't look at them. I tried to focus on his face.

Mom had a gash in her side. When I hugged her, she flinched. But she was worried about me, not herself. She asked me, "Are you okay? Have you eaten?"

She tried hard to soothe me. But she still had that lost look in her eyes. She gave me some of her hospital food, but I had no appetite.

Back at the crowded house, everyone treated us like we were about to break. No one knew how to talk to us. It was hard for me to feel much of anything. And I didn't want to feel anything anyway. The house was packed with people. The air was hot, suffocating. There was an outdoor toilet, which smelled atrocious with so many people using it.

We all shared mattresses. I had an impossible time sleeping. Darkness would descend and I would feel a blast of terror. Sometimes we heard gunfire in the distance, and my mind would go back to the camp and the gunshots that shook us from our beds. When I managed to sleep, I would wake up in the middle of the night, shaking uncontrollably. Shaking, shaking. I couldn't make it stop. My family thought I was going to die. They would cry, and I would cry. They tried to reassure me that I was safe. But I never felt safe.

My shaking got so bad, the entire house would wake up. I would shake for hours every night, then pass out around four thirty in the morning. I couldn't shed my terror of the dark. I dreaded going to bed. No one could snap me out of it.

This went on for weeks. I hated living like that, crippled by fear, but there was nothing I could do to stop it. There were days when I wished I had died in the camp. It simply hurt to be alive.

Our host family was so gracious; they tried really hard to help, caring for us generously when they had little room in their home. My family was kind of useless, too shell-shocked and upset to do anything. We could have gone to live in another refugee camp, but my parents said they would rather die than subject their kids to another camp.

Sadly, some members of our tribe had to go to another camp, because they had no other options. Imagine being sent to another camp after living through the hell of the first camp. I would not have survived in a new refugee camp. Every little noise would have terrorized me.

When Mom came home from the hospital, she was tiny. She had once been big and strong, confident and formidable. I didn't know it was possible for someone to become so little. I could see her getting smaller and smaller by the day.

Mom cried all the time. Everyone did. We would be sitting around, in our usual zoned-out state, and someone would suddenly cry. No one would question the reason for the tears. It was just part of our new life. Sometimes people would visit the house, look at us, and simply cry. There was no real conversation with any visitors, just crying. People didn't know how to be comforting. I remember women coming to the house to visit, to console us, and instead they would cry for hours at a time. Sometimes my mom would look at me and start to cry, and I wondered if it was because I had unknowingly done something—made a gesture or a facial expression—to remind her of Deborah. I worried that perhaps she resented me because I reminded her that her youngest child had died. I carried so much guilt.

There wasn't much food in the house, but we didn't want to eat it anyway.

The gloom continued for months. Finally, my dad said, "We need to get out of this country."

He thought if we moved out of Burundi, the land of the massacre, my mom and I would feel safer. We had a little money from donations that Good Samaritans gave to us in the hospital. And so in 2005, my dad put us on a bus and we moved to Rwanda.

There, we all crammed into a tiny rental apartment—my parents, Heritage, Princesse, Alex, and me—with just a bedroom and a half. We had an outhouse. The apartment was dark, like a dungeon. We had no furniture. There was no running water. We lived on top of each other. The landlord drank too much and would yell at us about nothing. We had a little joke among ourselves that he was such a drunk, his child's very first spoken word was "alcohol."

Adele and Chris, who had been in the mountains with my grandparents during the attack, eventually joined us. They brought along some money, which my grandparents had earned from selling a cow. Adele and Chris were disoriented. They didn't know whether they should talk to us about what happened in the massacre. And they were heartbroken at losing Deborah.

They had endured their own problems on their journey to reunite with us. First, they walked for three days from the mountains to Uvira, where the Congolese promptly poisoned them in a restaurant. After that, they went to stay with a friend of the family in Burundi so they could get medical care. Then they took a bus to our apartment in Rwanda. It had taken them three weeks to get to us.

Sometimes we went for days with no food or water. I understood for the first time how it felt to experience real poverty. To wash our clothes and clean the dishes, we would get water from a nearby pond. But the pond was polluted, so my mom needed to boil the water. For drinking water, sometimes Mom managed to get a jug of tap water from neighbors, or I would be dispatched to sit beneath a leaking pipe connected to another home. The pipe was at the bottom of a hill, and I would walk down there and huddle with other poor people from the neighborhood, collecting drips of water. There were a lot of desperate people waiting to get that water, including kids my age and mothers with babies. Arguments would erupt. It felt mortifying and also humbling to be among those people waiting for drips. I realized there were so many people struggling to survive. We were not the only ones.

My dad tried to find a job, but there was no work for

an undocumented refugee in Rwanda. We were foreigners again. We didn't sound Rwandan since we had never lived there—or even visited there—until now. Ironically, people back home in Congo had called us Rwandan, but here in Rwanda, people called us Congolese. We didn't fit in anywhere. We were stateless.

At night, Mom and Dad slept in the bedroom, and the rest of us slept on mats and blankets on the floor in the main room. Over time, my shaking started to get better. I was far away from where the attack had happened, so that helped, and also I didn't hear gunfire at night. My parents would ask us to pray. Dad kept a written list of things we should pray for—food, money, education, jobs. I remember thinking: God is not going to suddenly drop us some food and money.

But my parents never gave up. I had never thought much about religion or God, despite having grown up Christian. Eventually, seeing the unwavering faith of my parents, I began to open myself up to the idea of God's help. I prayed with Mom, morning and night. Sometimes we all prayed together as a family. Dad would call us together and pick someone to lead us in prayer. He liked to pick the younger kids.

"God listens more closely to children," Mom said.

I hoped she was right. Maybe there really is some sort of

higher power that can help us, I thought. I prayed all the time, even when I was alone. My faith began to deepen. I began to see that certain things were beyond my control, beyond my parents' control. I put my faith in God.

That faith would soon be shaken.

TWELVE

MY PARENTS THOUGHT IT MIGHT CHEER ME up if I could escape from our hovel and visit a cousin who lived a few hours away in East Africa. My cousin was older than me, married with kids. I adored her. Whenever she came to visit us in Congo, she looked stylish and hip, with perfect hair and high heels, and she would let me play with her makeup. I felt a flicker of excitement—the first since the massacre—about the prospect of getting away.

Soon I was on my way. When I arrived, the kids in the family welcomed me, treating me like any other kid. They didn't treat me like the girl who had just gone through a massacre. They made fun of me, which I appreciated—they didn't act like I was going to break.

The massacre came up only briefly, when I was playing in the yard with the youngest daughter, who was around two years younger than me.

"So you had a little sister, right?" she asked.

"Yes," I said abruptly, hoping we could move on. Her mother must have told her about Deborah.

"How old was she?"

"Six years old."

"Do you miss her?"

"Yeah, I miss her."

"My mom said you'll see her in heaven."

I kept quiet, ending the conversation there. I think she understood that I did not want to talk about it.

One day, she and I were hanging out together in the house when her father told her to go to the market. I will call her Ganza, although that is not her real name; I am protecting her identity because of what happened next.

I said I would go with Ganza to the market, but her father said no, I should stay. I didn't know why he wanted me to remain with him. Ganza headed out to do the shopping, and he and I were the only ones in the house.

As soon as his daughter left, he grabbed me and threw me onto his bed. I was shocked, confused. He kissed my face, hard, and rubbed himself up against me. In a panic, I pushed back and tried to fight him off. He was a strong man, and I was just a kid. He overpowered me and held me down, covering my mouth so I couldn't scream. He continued to rub his body against mine. He tried taking off my shorts, but I shut my legs tightly. He moved his hands up my bare chest as he continued to silence my screams with unwanted kisses. I had no idea what to do. In a culture where men feel entitled to take women, I knew that if he was successful in raping me, I could be discarded by my family, forced to marry because I was no longer a virgin. In many cultures, including mine, young women who are sexually abused are often blamed and rejected by their communities.

He continued to lay unwanted kisses on me as I struggled to escape his grip.

"Stay quiet," he said, as if I should lie there and let him take what he thought was his—my body.

And then, mercifully, we heard the front door. Ganza was home. He pushed me off the bed and I fell on the floor with a thud, crying. I had fought so hard that he had not managed to rape me. But the sexual assault at the hands of someone I loved and trusted left me shattered. I didn't understand why a grown man would want to attack a kid. He had a beautiful wife, an adult woman with curves. I hadn't even gone through puberty. And I had gone to this man's home to recuperate from the massacre, from seeing my little sister shot dead. I was in the most vulnerable state imaginable. This man was supposed to help me, not rape me. He said to keep my mouth shut or I would be sorry.

I didn't keep my mouth shut, at least not at first. Almost immediately, I told Ganza he had attacked me. Her response was devastating.

"Sandra, my father would never do anything like that," she said, in a chilling, matter-of-fact tone.

She didn't believe me, or maybe she didn't want to believe me. She was young, around nine years old. She could not accept that her father would do such a disgusting thing. I'm sure it made no sense to her, just as it made no sense to me. But it happened. She brushed me off and moved on to the next topic. We never discussed it again. She was the last person I told.

I was deeply embarrassed and ashamed, even though I had done nothing wrong. I thought that if I told my cousin what her husband had done, she wouldn't believe me either. And anyway, rape was not something we discussed in my culture. There was a culture of silence surrounding the crime.

There wasn't even really a word for "rape" in my native language. The closest phrasing would be something like, "He forcibly took me." It was a heavy load for a child to keep inside. But I kept it to myself. I locked it away.

I had to stay in that awful house for three more months. I made sure I was always in the company of someone else, never alone with that man. He pretended that nothing had happened. He did not attack me again, but I lay awake in fear at night, remembering the assault. He had shaken my trust to the core. I didn't know who to trust now. Strange men had killed my sister; a man I knew had attacked me. My life, my spirit, were crumbling.

When I finally went back to my family, I didn't tell anyone what had happened. I buried the experience deep down inside. But it kept rearing its ugly head, coming out in different ways. My attacker's actions changed the way I looked at older men, and at male relatives. If an older uncle or male cousin tried to hug me, I got fidgety and nervous. My mom noticed, but clearly did not know why. She probably thought it was one of my quirks. I tried to make sure I did not look attractive if older men came to our home.

I never did tell my mother, or anyone at all, about the attack. I thought I would keep that secret inside of me until I died.

I am telling the story for the first time now—in this book. It is incredibly difficult for me to tell this story. I thought for a long time about whether I should do it. I thought about how it would be painful for the man's children if they were to find out. I considered how it could hurt their relationship with their father. The man's wife has since left him, but the kids would not want to hear that their father is a pedophile. I thought about how they might not believe me, how they might call me a liar. I don't know if Ganza remembers the day I told her, all those years ago; my guess is that she buried it. She would be upset to hear this now. My community might be upset as well, because I am breaking the culture of silence. They might not understand why I would tell this story. My family might worry about my divulging something so personal.

But it is not my responsibility to protect a predator. I've stayed silent for nearly a decade, never telling a soul. He had counted on that. He had counted on the silence of a child, confused and embarrassed by the actions of a trusted adult. But I do not need to protect him any longer. He did this. He is a sexual predator, a pedophile who attacked a little girl. If it causes problems in his family to hear it, then he should have thought about that before he tried to rape me. I am the victim. He is the predator. If people want to blame me for telling the truth, that's their problem.

I have decided to tell this story because I have learned that I do have a voice. I do not want to be a part of this culture of silence. This book is my voice. I am telling my life story in these pages, and so I want to tell my full, authentic life story. So many girls around the world—refugee girls in particular—suffer in silence after being sexually assaulted by someone they know. Most rapes happen at the hands of a relative or friend, not a stranger. I want girls to know that they have the power to speak out. They don't have to stay quiet. No matter what culture or country you are from, there will always be pressure to remain silent, to never tell. But you don't have to protect sexual predators. By speaking up, you are standing up for yourself. And you might be preventing it from happening again. Tell people what happened. The predators expect you to stay silent. You can prove them wrong.

THIRTEEN

BACK WITH MY FAMILY IN OUR DIM LITTLE
shanty in Rwanda, we continued our struggle to survive.
There were many nights without dinner. My mom couldn't
afford to buy much food at the market, usually just a half
pound of beans, a few ingredients to make gravy, and some
cornstarch to make kaunga, a traditional doughlike dish. We
would each roll a piece of the kaunga into a little ball, then
dip it in gravy, until it was gone. We ate this all the time.
Alex made light of the situation, teasing my mom.

"Mom, here's an idea," he said. "What if one day you
skipped the beans and bought a half pound of meat instead?"

"Alex," Mom said. "You think I don't want to buy you meat?"

But then she thought about what he said, and she tried something new: She bought a small amount of chicken— a quarter pound—and mixed it with beans and cabbage. It was her own recipe, and a welcome change.

"This actually tastes better than beef!" Alex said.

Then he had another brilliant idea: He suggested that he and I should get more food than anyone else, since we were the youngest and had been eating for the least amount of time. "We need to catch up!" he said.

Alex always made us laugh, even on those dinnerless nights.

Sometimes a neighbor would stop by and bring us food or money. And one of my cousins in Burundi, Deborah Rose, helped as well. She started a small business selling clothes and brought us money when she could. Once when she came to visit, Mom sang a song about how God lifts people from the garbage and cleans and dresses them. My cousin found this song annoying.

"God doesn't do all that for you," she said. "How could you be singing that? You had such a good life, and look where you are now."

Still, Mom kept the faith. She believed that a lot of miracles happened in that home to keep us alive. My own faith had wavered. It was hard for me to see God at the time.

But Mom was right. Princesse got a scholarship for college in Kigali, the capital of Rwanda. She also got a job at a government minister's office, which was rare for an undocumented immigrant, but she had impressed her employers at the interview. She started bringing us money she earned on the job.

My family got involved with a local church, and my dad formed a choir with the kids in the congregation. We began singing in churches around the region. Dad suggested that we raise money from the performances to help educate kids from our tribe who had survived the massacre, and so we did.

Around this time, a man at church befriended my dad and took an interest in our family. He came to our home and talked with us, asking questions about our life. As it turned out, he was a director of a boarding school.

When I heard him say this, I said, "I need to go to school. I miss school!"

Mom gave me the stink eye for blurting out my personal desires to someone we hardly knew.

"You're not in school?" the man asked.

"No," I said. "I haven't been to school for a long time."

"We have scholarships at our school for smart students," he said.

"I'm the smartest student!" I said, unable to contain myself. "I'm really smart! I promise you, I would do well!"

Then my mom backed me up. "It's true," she said. "Sandra was always at the top of her class."

This kind man helped Alex and me get scholarships. Before long, my brother and I were on our way to boarding school, which was about three hours away by bus.

On the morning Mom escorted us to the bus stop, I could barely control my emotions. I was so eager to get to that school. Mom was busy giving us all kinds of advice.

"Be careful," she said. "Study hard. Always tell the principal if something is wrong."

I nodded. "Yes, yes, yes." I couldn't wait for the bus to come and take me to school, finally.

And then I was back in uniform—this time, khaki shorts and a white shirt. The school was small and intimate, perched in the mountains. The weather was cooler than we were used to, especially in the mornings and evenings, but it was a heavenly oasis. We spoke French there and fit right in. Alex and I made friends quickly.

I stayed in touch with my parents by phone and saw them on trimester breaks. My older siblings Chris and Adele went back to school as well. And Dad got a job in the church. We were coming back to life.

Toward the end of 2005, about a year and a half after the massacre, Dad heard a rumor about a United Nations resettlement program for people who had survived the massacre at our camp in Gatumba. There was a chance we could move to America. But it would mean a series of interviews with UN workers in Burundi, the home of the massacre, and my mom didn't want to go. There were too many horrendous memories there. She also found it hard to believe that we could get to America with the help of white people; it seemed like an impossible dream. I was equally skeptical. I didn't think anyone cared that my people had been killed.

"Why don't we just find out if this thing is real?" Dad said.

"If it's real, why don't they come to us?" Mom said.

In 2006, my dad went to the first two interviews in Burundi alone.

After the interviews, he rounded us all up, including my reluctant mom, to travel to Burundi for the next round of interviews. Dad convinced Mom to go by telling her, "If it doesn't work out, we'll come back. But if it does work out, then our kids deserve a better life, don't they? We should give them that opportunity. Why not try?"

At the UN office in Burundi, we sat in a crowded room with other families from the massacre, our first reunion. It felt good to see my people, but sad too. Everyone had lost loved ones, and no one looked quite the same as they had in our happier years in Uvira. It was like an eerie dream, seeing faces of ghosts from the past. People looked older, although not much time had passed.

The workers in the office were all white, and I saw an obese woman for the first time. I had never seen anyone so heavy. An American, she wore a blue shirt and black pants, and she spoke in a no-nonsense tone. She rattled off a list of questions with the help of a translator.

"How many people are in your family?"

"How old is everyone?"

"Tell me everyone's birth dates."

Then she asked, "How many people did you lose?"

This question seemed so matter-of-fact, so emotionless. We had lost our beloved Deborah. Her violent death had left a hole in our family that would never be repaired. We had lost cousins, aunts, uncles, and friends.

I understood that the woman was doing her job. She was resettling people from our massacre, and she needed to make sure the right people were being relocated. But she did not seem to understand that we were grieving. Our world had been turned upside down, and now we had to retell our horror story. I saw no empathy; she was recording facts. My mom was having a difficult time talking about Deborah as if she were a statistic. After that, Mom said she didn't want to go to America.

My dad, however, said we should keep trying. We went in for another round of interviews, and this time, we were all separated in different rooms, with officials asking us questions individually. Since I was young, my mom was allowed to sit with me during my interview. I feared that if my answers didn't match up precisely with those of my family, we would not get to go to America. I didn't want to blow it for my family, although I still found it hard to believe that any of this was real. I didn't know how to feel about moving to the States—I just knew that I needed to say consistent things and not mess up. But people don't always recall the same details from traumatic situations. I had noticed this from the members of my own family: We were in the same massacre, but we sometimes had differ-ent recollections.

An official asked me a long list of questions.

"Where were you born?"

"Who are your parents?"

"How many siblings do you have? How old are they?"

"What are their names?"

"When did you go to the refugee camp in Gatumba?"

"Where were you the night of the attack? Who were you with?"

"Who survived?"

I was nervous as I answered, even though I knew the answers well.

My mom was nervous too, and she managed to mix up some of our birth dates. I was born on June 22, but in her anxiety-ridden state, Mom said it was June 1. Because of that, my birthday is now officially June 1.

During this time, most of us stayed with relatives or friends in Burundi so we would be available for the interviews. Mom and Princesse stayed in Rwanda, traveling back and forth for the interviews. Mom wanted to spend as little time in Burundi as possible. Sometimes the UN officials would pay the rest of us a surprise visit in Burundi and ask questions about our family, again checking that we were who we said we were.

"Where is everyone sleeping?" they would ask. "There don't seem to be enough beds."

We would explain that when you lose everything, you can't afford much of anything. This went on for months. We waited, answered questions, waited some more. You really have to want to get to America to put yourself through the process. Anyone who thinks it's easy to get to the States as a refugee has no idea.

Finally, we got the news: Our application had been accepted. We would be resettled in America. For me, it was a bittersweet moment. I knew we would have new opportunities in America. But at the same time, we would be leaving behind our life in Africa, everything we had ever known. We would be saying good-bye to people we loved—other families from the massacre who were still waiting to hear their fate. I had the uneasy feeling that we were abandoning them, as if we had the magic ticket and they did not. We did not know where we would be living in America. And we did not know the date of our move, so it still seemed like an unattainable concept, not a reality.

As we awaited our departure date, we continued to live in our temporary circumstances, in limbo. I was staying with a family in Burundi, not going to school, and so I spent my time helping to babysit the kids in the family. For weeks, our move to America continued to feel unreal—until the officials took us to a health clinic, where we got tested for things like HIV and tuberculosis. That's when we knew we were really going.

My family began attending classes to learn about life in America. We watched videos and listened to advice from a caseworker, with the help of a translator. I didn't learn much about America during these sessions: Mostly I learned that it was cold and snowy. We watched a lot of videos that showed piles of snow. I had never experienced snow before. I remember the translator giving us this piece of advice as well: "When you get to America, don't stare at people. Don't point."

I thought that was funny. As if we would go around staring and pointing at people!

And then one day, we got some solid information on our departure for the States: Heritage would go first, and I would follow with my parents and Alex. Then Princesse and Chris would go. We were scheduled to go at different times, not as a family unit, because the UN handles people who are over the age of eighteen as individual cases. Since Alex, Adele, and I were under eighteen, we were grouped with our parents.

In April 2007, my time came.

My parents, Alex, Adele, and I packed our suitcases for the journey of our lives, not that we had much of anything to pack. Dad, who had saved the shirt and belt riddled with bullet holes from the massacre, left them behind.

With our few bags of belongings, we went to a hotel in Burundi, where we stayed for a week with other families who would be relocated. It was our last week in Africa. We were finally going to America, to a city in New York called Rochester. Heritage would be there waiting for us.

I didn't really know how to picture America. I had no solid frame of reference, no true mental image of the place.

I had the general impression that in addition to being freezing cold and snowy all the time, it was a land where people were happy and rich. That's the idea I had gotten from the UN caseworkers, and from anything I had ever seen on TV over the years. I also figured there were a lot of white people there. I had the feeling that nothing bad ever happened to people in America. The caseworkers painted a picture of America as a dream, the land of opportunity.

I thought that once we got to America, everything would be fine. Little did I know.

FOURTEEN

THE AIRPLANE WAS HUGE, THE BIGGEST thing I had ever been inside of that was not a house. As my family boarded the enormous vessel, I had many burning questions for my parents.

"Where do we pee?"

"What about food?"

A flight attendant showed us the bathrooms, and I thought: Where does the pee go when we're in the sky? Does it land on people's heads?

Other questions churned in my brain. How are there lights on the plane? How can there be electricity in the sky?

I didn't see any wires, any outlets. I had never flown before. It was all a mystery.

When the plane took off, the engines roared like a beast. As we sliced upward through the sky, I looked out the window at the vanishing ground below, and thought: Oh my god, we are going to fall. It seemed as if the plane was too heavy to fly. My dad looked out at the wings, with their flaps moving up and down.

"I don't think the wings are working!" he said.

The plane began to rattle and rock from choppy air. Mom gripped her seat, bracing herself. The look on her face said: What have we gotten ourselves into?

Once we rose above the clouds, no longer bumping around in the turbulence, the excitement set in and I started having fun. We were flying to a new life on the other side of the world.

"This is like a dream," Dad said.

He was thrilled to be able to give his family this opportunity. We had been struggling for so long. He told us that in America, we would not necessarily fit in, but that we had a chance to better ourselves and further our education.

Other families from the massacre were on the plane with us, and people were in good spirits, if a little discombobulated. Because everything was labeled in English, some people got confused and sprinkled packets of salt in their tea instead of sugar. Someone ate a pat of butter. We shared some laughs about that.

I was astounded that there was a kitchen on the plane, serving up warm food. A few people got motion sickness, and threw up in barf bags. Alex and I discovered that we could entertain ourselves by running up and down the aisles.

We had a layover in Kenya, then in London. The London airport was swirling with people. Announcements blared from speakers in crisp British accents. For a snack, I tasted an apple for the first time. I took a bite and thought it was the nastiest thing—it was soft and squishy, not crisp. This is fruit? I thought. This is disgusting!

Dad tried it too, and I was impressed that he kept eating it beyond the first bite.

Mom laughed. "Do you actually like it?" she asked.

"No," he said. "But I have to get used to the food."

We all laughed. My dad, such a trooper.

Finally, we flew into John F. Kennedy International Airport in New York City—and landed in the middle of a snowstorm. Looking out the window at the wild gusts of snowflakes, I thought: Oh my goodness, these people live in ice.

The airport was massive, like a humongous maze, over-flowing with people. Some slept on the floor with their luggage, awaiting delayed flights. It was startlingly cold, even though we were indoors. The heating system couldn't keep up with the weather, and we had no winter coats. I was wearing a thin pink jogging suit. We retrieved our bags, and Mom pulled out her traditional cotton dresses. We wrapped them around us, trying to add layers of warmth. She kept pulling out more clothes for all of us. We definitely stood out. Mom's frocks were made in the brightly patterned East African fabrics known as kitenge, or igitenge. I didn't see any other people from Africa, except for the people in our own group. I had never seen so many white faces in my life.

We needed to find our connecting flight to Rochester, which was challenging because none of us spoke English. But we had the entire day to get to the departure gate. The snow had delayed all the flights. My dad showed people his ticket, and we eventually made our way to the gate, weaving our way through the obstacle course of people lying on the floor. We boarded the plane for the final leg of our journey, a short flight to northern New York.

When we arrived in Rochester, dawn was breaking. Heritage stood there in the airport, waiting for us with a big smile. He was with a caseworker, a Ukrainian woman named Katarina, and a new friend he had met, a refugee from Uganda named Jacob. We stepped outside the airport to go to the car, and the arctic wind stopped us.

"I feel like I'm being electrocuted," Dad said.

We got our bearings and hurried to the car, shivering to the core. As we drove through the streets of Rochester, I looked out the window and saw a city covered in white. The snow coated everything—houses, yards, treetops, churches, cars. Nobody was outside. It seemed like I was in a strange, hazy dream. We stopped at a run-down house in an inner-city neighborhood that we were told served as temporary housing for refugees.

I was so worn out from our hours in the sky, it was hard to focus on much of anything, but I remember thinking that the house looked kind of old and beat-up, its paint chipping. Even as a twelve-year-old girl landing in America for the first time, I could sense that we were not in a nice neighborhood. Of course, it was surely better than being crammed into a one-room apartment with my entire family in Rwanda. But it was also disappointing: I had been promised the American dream. It was my first hint that life in America might not be such a dream after all.

The house was stocked with food I had never seen before, like peanut butter. I thought peanut butter was an especially odd concept: You were supposed to cook with peanuts, not pound them into a cream to put in a jar. There were more apples. There was no whole milk. We grew up on whole milk, gulping it down every day. When I opened the refrigerator, I hollered for my mother.

"Mom, these people eat worms!" I said, pointing to a package of pink worms.

"No, no," she said, shaking her head.

"Look!"

She looked at the piles of worms, confused, just like me. We learned later that it was ground beef.

Those first few days were strange and disorienting. It was frigid outside, so we mostly stayed indoors, catching up with Heritage and eating bread and drinking tea. We didn't have any other food we were used to eating, like chicken, vegetables, or our coveted whole milk. The microwave was another enigma: We wondered how it cooked food, since it didn't grill or fry. A caseworker brought us a TV, but the shows were in English, so we couldn't understand anything. I watched cartoons—*Arthur, Clifford the Big Red Dog.* I was too old for them, but they were the only shows I could under-stand. They turned out to be a good tool for learning English.

Our caseworkers tried to figure out what kinds of foods we liked, but communication was difficult. They bought us things like heavy cream for coffee, but we didn't drink coffee. I tasted the heavy cream and I thought: Ugh, this must be how milk tastes in America! They brought us chicken, but it tasted strange, probably from the hormones injected to make the birds fatter. Back home, we always ate fresh chicken, no chemicals. Mom wanted to prepare the chicken the way she always did for us, with her sauces and spices, and she tried to convey the ingredients she needed to the caseworkers. They genuinely tried. It just didn't work out. Mom would say she needed tomato paste for sauces, and they would come back with canned tomatoes instead. They would bring us things like onions and salt, which were not ingredients that she used. Mom would say, "What do I do with these?" Even when she got the spices she liked, the chicken tasted different than it did in Africa. I began to hate meat. Gradually, I stopped eating it all together.

We had a caseworker named John who thought it would help if he took us along with him to go food shopping at Walmart. It seemed logical enough; we could point out what we needed. John was a nice guy, an older man, worryingly overweight. I wondered if something was wrong with him. I didn't understand how he could get so big, or how he could survive in that unhealthy state. He drove us to the Walmart and we walked in the front door, where he promptly sat down on a little cart to drive himself around the aisles of the store. It seemed like no one walked anywhere. I thought: Is this a thing here? Nobody walks in America? You drive to the grocery store and then get out and drive around the store in a cart?

People in the store looked huge to me. The store was huge. I had been to big food markets in Rwanda, but Walmart was a new ball game—more like a town than a market, with its aisles and aisles of mysterious foods, like boxes of cereal. Cereal made no sense to me. I thought: You're supposed to put these flakes in a bowl of milk and eat them? What? Milk is for drinking!

There were aisles of cookies, potato chips, sweet snacks, salty snacks, bags of candy, and cheese presliced into little cubes and squares. The people at Walmart didn't look like the people I saw on TV. The people on TV—the models and actors—were super-skinny, especially the young women. They were rail thin, and they paraded around half naked in bikinis and short-shorts. I wondered where those people lived. Clearly not in Rochester.

We went to Walmart a few more times with John, and the trips remained uneasy. There was always a degree of tension as we tried to communicate what we needed: We didn't want to appear rude or ungrateful, but we didn't want to buy food that we would not eat. We hated to see food go to waste. We knew that food was a precious commodity. We rarely had translators to help us navigate anything, unless we had an official meeting of some sort. There were no other members of our tribe in Rochester. Everything was new to me. My brain could hardly process anything. My family was really flying blind.

FIFTEEN

OUR NEIGHBORHOOD WAS MOSTLY BLACK, but there were still more white people there than I had ever seen. Sometimes I saw the white people eyeing my family curiously. As we strolled the aisles in Walmart, I could tell they were talking about us, but I couldn't make out what they were saying. We definitely looked different: I was thin and wore my hair cropped very short, practically shaved, per the style for kids back home. I didn't see any girls in Rochester wearing their hair that way. My mom wore her traditional, vividly patterned African dresses.

The houses on our street were all very close together, but none of our neighbors came over and introduced themselves.

No one knocked on our door. Mom was surprised by how lonely and isolated America felt. The neighbors didn't seem to know each other. People locked their doors. Everyone kept to themselves. Mom would look out the window and ask, "Where are all the people?"

Back home on our sunny, friendly street in Uvira, we had people coming and going in our house all the time. People smiled and said hello when they passed you on the street. We never locked our doors.

One day, our caseworker John took us to a church clothing drive to help us stock up on clothes, including much-needed winter coats and boots. Adele had arrived at that point, and as we looked at the shelves of musty clothes, arranged by category—shirts, jeans, shoes—we couldn't help but giggle.

"Check out these pants," I said, pointing to a polyester pair that had not been popular for decades. They were universally unfashionable—not retro chic, just old, and they smelled old too.

Adele laughed. "Those bell bottoms are so big, you could use them as mops."

We spotted a long denim skirt, sending us into a new round of giggles.

"The only place someone could wear that skirt would be to an Ugly Skirt Convention," I said.

I didn't want to appear rude, but as a preteen girl, I thought, I wouldn't be caught dead wearing anything in here. Yes, we were refugees, but it didn't mean we had no fashion sense. Back home in Congo, our clothes were tailored, and they fit beautifully. People in America seemed to assume that we were coming from an undeveloped land where we had no decent clothes. But we knew style. And we had seen plenty of American music videos. We knew what Americans wore. I didn't want to get bullied out of school in Rochester for wearing a voluminous denim skirt.

I was also astonished by the array of short-shorts on offer at the clothing drive. The ladies who worked there pointed them out to me, encouraging me to pick them up. I had no interest in those shorts, and I could never wear them anyway: My dad would literally chop both my legs off if he saw me wearing them. And the shoes! Another bummer. Mainly they were heavy winter boots for trudging through snow, as ugly as could be. I wondered how people could wear those things. I figured it must be necessary to keep your feet from freezing off.

"Those shoes are like boats," Alex said.

We chose some boots and coats, out of necessity, and I also managed to take home two T-shirts and a pair of jeans—not stylish but wearable. John was surprised that we didn't take more items. He thought we would scoop up everything in sight. Another disconnect. I think people have this perception that because you're a refugee, you'll take anything you can get your hands on. To some extent that's true—we were definitely in need—but we are all just people. And everyone wants to look good, especially twelve-year-old girls. Girls are girls everywhere.

John tried again later, taking us to another clothing drive. He asked the women who worked there to find us superstylish things.

"These girls are very trendy," he said.

Actually, we weren't so fashionable; we were just regular girls. But we appreciated his efforts, and we tried to find some things, which remained a challenge. We noticed at both clothing drives that the clothes had a distinct smell: damp and moldy, like they'd been stored for a long time in wet cardboard boxes. Sometimes the clothes smelled like a hospital, perhaps from being stored in mothballs.

We began to wonder if this was how white people smelled.

My first real interaction with white kids came when I met two little girls who lived next door. They quietly wandered over one day when I was kicking around a ball with Alex in our backyard. The girls were around four and five years old, and they wanted to play. Pretty soon, they were hanging out in our home all the time. They appeared to be lonely, curious. Their mom drank alcohol and smoked, and the kids smelled like smoke too. It didn't help our growing suspicions that white people didn't smell so good.

As I got to know the girls, I remember thinking: Wow, I'm playing with white kids! Their mom seemed worried that the girls wanted to spend so much time with us—sometimes they would fall asleep in our house at night—but my mom welcomed their presence. She loved opening her home to others and having people around. To her, it was normal.

My two young friends had mountains of toys in their house. Dolls, stuffed animals, and plastic cars and trucks were strewn across the living room, and the kids didn't seem interested in any of them. They had an assortment of Barbie dolls, which struck me as particularly bizarre toys. The dolls were stick-thin, like the actresses on TV, unlike the people I saw in real life in Rochester. I thought it was weird that the Barbies wore makeup too. Actually I thought it was strange that the dolls had faces at all. My soft cloth dolls back home in Africa had no faces; we used our imagination to dream up their facial features and personalities.

The boobs on the Barbies were another matter. I thought they were so inappropriate! They actually made me uncomfortable. I wondered why kids would want to play with dolls that were so developed. The dolls seemed like they were made for adults, not kids. Children don't have gigantic boobs. Why did their dolls have them?

After just a couple weeks in Rochester, I began another weird new adventure: middle school in America.

SIXTEEN

I THOUGHT IT WAS STRANGE THAT I WOULD be sent to school so soon after landing in Rochester. It was April and there were just two months left in the school year. I didn't speak English, and I didn't feel ready. But the caseworkers thought it would be good for me to jump right in.

I was supposed to be in eighth grade, as I had finished seventh grade in Rwanda. But in America, I got placed in sixth grade. I had worked so hard on my education, and this felt like a setback. I knew I was being demoted because I didn't speak English, but this made me angry. How would being in a lower grade help me learn English? I didn't think our caseworkers valued the education we had achieved. Adding to my frustration, Alex would get to be in eighth grade—the grade I was supposed to be in.

My first day of school was the worst. I didn't know what to wear because I had always worn uniforms to school back home. My frumpy clothing-drive clothes embarrassed me. I wore bleached blue jeans, a generic striped green-and-white shirt, and white sneakers. I was very skinny, and the jeans were too baggy.

The school, John Williams School No. 5, was huge compared with my elementary school in Congo. This one had several floors and indoor bathrooms. Several bathrooms on each floor! I wondered why the students needed so many toilets. The bathrooms were clean, and filled with kids, gabbing and gossiping. Back home in Congo, I avoided using the school bathrooms because they were unsanitary and often lacked toilet paper. Students who were late or who misbehaved in class were responsible for the upkeep of the toilets at school. In my new school, it appeared that there were employees whose sole job was to clean up after the kids. I had so many questions.

The halls were chaotic, swarming with chattering, shouting kids. Lockers were always slamming. I saw some boys taunting an overweight girl. Discipline clearly did not rule the day, as it did in schools back home. I couldn't understand the words that anyone around me said. It was the first time I had been in a school where I could not comprehend anything at all. The kids stared at me. They were mostly black and Hispanic. No one said hello to me or smiled. I felt like an alien. I immediately wanted to turn around and go back to my family.

In class, my teacher, Ms. Wilson, didn't know what to do with me because of the language barrier, and she plunked down some math problems in front of me. Math was familiar to me, so that was one small comfort—numbers are numbers. Once in a while, the teacher would come and check up on me. She would speak slower and a bit louder than necessary, maybe because she thought it would help me. I sympathized with her—she was trying to do an impossible job: She was not an English-as-a-second-language teacher.

I was floored by how obnoxious the kids were. There was no chief of class to keep the peace when the teacher left the room. And even when the teacher was present, I could tell the kids were rude. They talked back to her. They smirked and made faces. They ignored her, texting on their phones while she spoke. Kids appeared to think of school as a chore, a bore. I thought of the boys back in Congo who were forced to serve as child soldiers, and the girls who were married off, never given a chance to finish high school. School is a privilege.

Another thing I didn't understand: why kids would need their own cell phones. So many kids had phones. I could see why adults might need them, but kids?

At lunchtime in the cafeteria, a new minefield: rows and rows of tables and chairs, cliques of friends, trays of weird food. I didn't know what to eat. I grabbed a little carton of milk and some fruit that looked familiar—an orange, a banana. I sat down at a table by myself. I had once loved going to school, and now I just wanted to go home. A boy named Abdul was the only kid to approach me. He was small in stature and seemed quiet, but with a mischievous air. He spoke to me in French, as kids from Africa generally know some French.

"Where are you from?" he asked.

"Congo," I said, relieved that someone was talking to me.

"I'm from Senegal," he said. "I speak a little French. I can try to help you understand what people are saying."

Abdul and I struck up an instant friendship. Ms. Wilson sat me next to him in class. He would quietly tell me what the teacher was talking about during the lessons, doing his best to use French. He would also translate for Ms. Wilson when she needed to communicate something directly to me. Abdul was helpful, but it should not have been his responsibility to make sure I was learning in school.

Those first days of school were a perplexing blur, but I remember the feeling clearly: pure misery. I looked different from the other students with my buzz-cut hair and used clothes, and I wanted desperately to blend in. I wanted long hair. None of the black girls wore their hair short like mine. No one wore their hair in its natural state either. The girls straightened or relaxed their hair, or wore long braids or weaves. Some wore head scarves. I needed long hair. I needed braids.

Fortunately, the semester was drawing to a close. In June, I escaped the dreaded school for the summer. I shed my winter coat, mittens, and boots. I hated those boots. In fact, I hated shoes in general. I had spent my childhood wearing flip-flops—my feet felt free. Shoes trap you. You always have to take them off, put them back on, tie the laces—so much effort. I'd much rather be in flip-flops. I was thrilled that summer had come. I was learning a little English from watching TV, especially the cartoons, which were easy to follow. I would listen to the words and watch the facial expressions and reactions to figure out what things meant. I tried to muster some optimism that the next school year would be better.

My family left our temporary housing for a house in another inner-city neighborhood, which seemed even rougher and poorer than the first. We had a dilapidated blue home with two stories, four bedrooms, and creaky stairs. If you walked downstairs at night, you woke up the entire household. It was an immigrant neighborhood, mostly black and Hispanic.

The neighbor kids threw rocks at us. They called us nasty names, like "bootie scratcher." They made fun of my short hair, calling me a boy or claiming I had cancer. I couldn't always understand the insults, but you can tell from people's body language when they're saying something crude. One time Alex attempted to communicate to a mother that her kids were harassing us and calling us names. To try to explain, he made a rock-throwing motion with his arm. She dismissed him and allowed her kids to keep doing it. Where was our American dream?

I began to realize that maybe it didn't matter where you lived in the world, that people are people everywhere, not so different after all.

We were not prepared for the inner city. The caseworkers had taught us how to call 911, and we learned how to write our address on a piece of paper in case we got lost. My family had also been warned not to go out after dark, but we didn't understand why. None of us knew the range of dangers that lurked in a desperate neighborhood. I had thought we would be safe in America. We had a home phone but no cell phones. We were vulnerable, although we didn't know it.

There was a group of older guys who hung out on our street, and they always made a point to talk to me. They would say, "Oh, you're so pretty!" I would reply quietly, "Thank you." In my culture, you're not supposed to ignore people who are older than you. You're supposed to speak to them. It felt wrong not to respond. But they put me on edge. I had not forgotten what another man had done to me. Thankfully, these guys never gave me any trouble beyond the catcalling.

The neighborhood was plagued with crime, and sometimes the police would come in their cruisers, sirens blasting. The first time I saw the officers, with their guns and uniforms, I thought there must be a war on the way. Back in Congo, police officers and military officers were basically the same—and they came when there was war. They didn't make house calls about fights or loud noise. Eventually, I got used to the police presence in Rochester. I was relieved that we didn't have to flee our home for safety.

One bright spot in our neighborhood was a little store run by a Jamaican family, selling clothing, hair accessories, and other items. The Jamaicans were always kind to us. They seemed to understand how to deal with people who weren't American. They didn't mock or shun us. They were relaxed, friendly people, always willing to chat, unlike the Americans in our neighborhood, who seemed more closed off. I liked to tag along with my brothers to the shop and hang out.

My parents, meanwhile, were looking for a Christian church, specifically a Free Methodist church like the one we had attended in Africa. We went to different churches on Sundays to try them out, even though we couldn't understand what anyone was saying. We wanted to find a church we loved. And then we found the New Hope Church, and our prayers were answered.

The first time we went, we were greeted warmly, and we felt right at home. But we were perplexed at how short the service was. In Africa, you go to church on Sunday knowing you're not going to get out until the sun goes down. Nobody makes plans on a Sunday back home. It's all about church, all day. In America, the service was just about an hour and a half long. But I was into it—no all-day church! The service was also surprisingly quiet and mellow. Back home, church is loud.

Pastor Linda, a white woman, quickly became one of my favorite people. She was compassionate and kind, and she and my mom became good friends, even though they couldn't communicate well. They seemed to have a deep understanding and respect for each other.

Linda began driving us to and from church every Sunday.

If my family needed anything, the church members were there to help, taking my mom shopping or helping us run errands. Linda advised me to stay alert in my neighborhood and to always be sure to tell my mom where I was going. I took her advice, even though it seemed odd. Back in Africa, I didn't tell my mom every time I went somewhere. There, everyone knew everyone on the block. If Mom didn't know where I was and needed me for some reason, she could easily find me. All she had to do was step outside and ask around. She would find me in about five seconds.

My parents were having a difficult time parenting in America because they didn't know the language or the culture. I began asking Linda things I would ordinarily ask them, like about words and phrases I had heard people use. Her kids were grown, and she spent a lot of time with my siblings and me, answering questions, helping us with homework, offering advice. She was a calming voice. My family trusted her. She liked to sing, and she taught me a song called "Blessed Be Your Name." It was the first song I learned in English. One day, she and Princesse and I were singing it with her in her living room, and I started to cry.

There was a refrain in the song that made me think of Deborah: "You give and take away. You give and take away. My heart will choose to stay. Lord, blessed be your name."

"What's the matter?" Linda asked me.

"I don't know," I said.

But she was so warmhearted, I decided to confide in her that I missed my little sister. Linda didn't know exactly what had happened to Deborah, but she consoled me, saying, "God has a plan, even though you can't see it at the moment." Her guidance and faith were soothing to me. She reminded me of all the wonderful things I loved about church and community. I thought about how being Christian doesn't mean that everything is perfect all the time, or that you don't face any struggles. In that moment, I really thought about what God meant to me personally. I had been angry at him, but I decided to give him another chance.

Linda found an African market and tried to help us get the spices and foods we liked. She would do research and bring us different kinds of foods, asking, "Do you eat this?" One day, she took Adele and me shopping in a mall and let us pick out clothes. I loved the mall, so sleek and flashy, filled with shoppers and treasures. This is awesome, I thought. And the clothes didn't smell.

On Sundays after church, Linda sometimes drove us over to her house for a visit. She lived on the bank of a lake, in a beautiful neighborhood with fancy houses and perfect green lawns. I didn't have to be a genius to notice that the

white-people neighborhood was much nicer than our neighborhood. I didn't understand why our neighborhood felt
more dangerous than hers. I wondered if it truly was more
dangerous, or if it just felt that way. And if indeed it was
more dangerous, what was the reason?

One afternoon, Alex took a kayak out on the lake at
Linda's house by himself, and so, as usual, I followed his
lead. I jumped in my own kayak, thinking if he could sail the
lake, so could I. But I had no idea what I was doing. I drifted
out too far and couldn't get the kayak turned around. I kept
floating farther and farther out. The water out there was too
deep for me to swim back, and I started crying. Mom was
calling to me from the shore. She was crying too, and I'm
sure she was thinking: We didn't come all this way for you
to drown in this lake.

Linda sent some people out in a speedboat to pick me up
and bring me back ashore. I think it was a sign of things to
come.

SEVENTEEN

THE TAUNTS FROM KIDS IN MY NEIGHBORHOOD
continued, mainly focused on my short hair. The kids made
me cry, and I could not make my hair grow fast enough
to stop the insults. I hated to step outside the front door.
To shield myself from the jeers, I decided I needed a wig.
I wanted to fit in and look like everyone else. I thought the
wig would be the answer to my problems. I started talking
about it all the time to my parents.

"All the kids have hair," I said. "They think I'm a boy."

I kept making a fuss about it. Anytime we went to a store
and I saw a wig or extensions, I would point them out, ever
so hopefully. My parents didn't seem to get why this was

important to me. So I kept talking about it. Finally, an uncle who had recently resettled in America told me, "Okay, let's go." He took me to a beauty salon, and we found a cheap wig—curly black synthetic hair. It made my scalp and the back of my neck itch like mad. It gave me rashes on my skin. But I felt so much better about myself when I wore it. I endured the scratchiness and dressed it up with headbands and scarves.

The idea of beauty in America was new to me, and it was troublesome. The message I heard everywhere—from television, from people at school—was that I should exercise and eat healthy food so that I could stay skinny. Back home in Congo, we didn't really think about body size. Most people I knew were at a healthy weight. And being skinny was not something a child aspired to be. I started to feel pressure to look like what America considered beautiful. My dad helped me navigate the turmoil.

"Beauty is in your head, not on your body," Dad would say.

He never ceased to tell me about the importance of education. He said to stay focused on my schooling, not to get caught up in nonsense. If I skipped a meal, he lectured me, telling me I shouldn't listen to outsiders and their skewed views on beauty. If I worried about my hair, he said, "You are beautiful with short hair, without any alterations to the way you were made." My dad is probably the reason that I am a feminist. His voice was a powerful one, though I couldn't help but listen to the voices at school and on TV.

I found a few kindred spirits in the church youth group. The kids there didn't want to kill me—how novel! They actually wanted to get to know me. I became friends with a girl named Mabel, a white girl who was intelligent and tried valiantly to speak with me, even though I still knew little English. She worked with me, helping to teach me some words. I began to think maybe America wasn't so bad. Maybe there was hope.

For my thirteenth birthday in June, a woman from our church named Rosemary threw me a party. We didn't really do birthday parties or birthday cake back home. Birthdays weren't a big thing. In Congo, we celebrated major holidays, such as Christmas and Easter, not birthdays. And I didn't love cake. It tasted so sweet and, well, cakey. But the party was generous, and I appreciated the gesture. Rosemary helped me pick out a white dress and red heels for the party. I wore my new outfit and wig, feeling spiffy. She had four daughters, and I hung out with the younger ones at the party, even though we had some communication challenges. I was touched by how many people came to celebrate with me.

That summer, I practiced English by watching cartoons,

and spent as much time as I could with the youth group. I was surprised at how hot the summer months were, when the winter months had been so frigid. Everything felt extreme in America. But I was still gleeful at being free of the coats.

Mabel rapidly became my best friend. She invited me everywhere and helped me feel like I belonged. One night, she invited me over to her suburban home for a slumber party. Her house was enchanting. The kids each had their own individual bedrooms, full of their favorite things. I had never had a room to myself. Each bedroom had its own personality. In her room, Mabel had posters of her favorite singers plastered across the walls, along with piles of brightly colored yarn everywhere, since she was in a bracelet-making phase.

Mabel seemed truly interested in my life. She had some inkling about my past from the older people at church, who knew we were refugees, but she never pushed me to talk about it. She was waiting for me to do it in my own time. And that night, I confided in her. We sat in her bedroom and I found myself opening up, telling my life story, or as much as I could communicate. I didn't give her all of the atrocious details, but I expressed how sad I was.

Even within my own family, we hadn't really spoken about the massacre. We hadn't talked about Deborah. It was too painful, too fresh. No one knew how to bring it up, or the language to use. I had never said aloud that Deborah had died. At Mabel's sleepover, I said it for the first time. Mabel had made me feel comfortable and loved. She was my closest friend, and I knew she would support me, no matter what I said or did. And then I started crying, and couldn't stop. Saying the words out loud to another person made it more real, more permanent. I knew, of course, that Deborah had been gunned down, but I still had some vague, inexplicable sense that she would come back one day, as if she had taken a trip somewhere.

I hadn't yet opened my mind up to the past. My brain wasn't ready to process it. I had been too busy trying to survive after the attack, moving to America, attempting to navigate middle school. My family had never had any kind of therapy to deal with the trauma. I struggled to accept that the massacre was real, that all those people died in the camp, that kids were killed or orphaned.

Mabel tried hard to make me feel at home on the night I told my story, and I appreciated her kindness. We formed a lifetime bond during that slumber party.

My parents were trying to find their way as well. They both got jobs in a factory, packaging clothes. They learned how to take a city bus back and forth. Early on, Mom got lost and had to write down her address to show people, so they could point her home. The factory hours were long and tiring, and the work was tedious. It was painful to see my parents come home looking so worn out. But they never complained. They did what they had to do.

I hated seeing them that way. I thought about how Mom had run her own business in Congo, how Dad had always held good jobs. It was a wake-up call for all of us: As refugees in America, we were at the bottom of the heap. Your credentials from your home country don't matter. You could come here with a college education, like Princesse did, and it wouldn't mean anything. She had studied international relations in college in Rwanda. She had held a job in the government. But it didn't count in America. She would have to go to college again. People in America don't care about college degrees or careers from Africa. Princesse had worked so hard to get that education. We had been through so much to get our golden ticket to America. But we were invisible.

And then one night, just before I was due to start seventh grade, our world turned upside down again. It was a warm August evening, just turning dark, and my dad got on his bike to go pay the electric bill. He should have been back home quickly, but he wasn't. My mom began to worry.

"Where is he?" she kept asking. "Where could he be?"

We all stayed up late, sitting in the living room, waiting. Dad didn't have a phone with him. We couldn't imagine where he had gone.

He did not come back.

EIGHTEEN

THE POLICE KNOCKED ON OUR DOOR AROUND one o'clock in the morning, while I was asleep. I awoke the next morning to hear the news. Princesse said the police had come and tried to talk to Mom, but she couldn't understand them. Mom had called for Princesse, who spoke the best English because she had studied it in college. The officers told Princesse that our dad had been in an accident. A van had hit him while he was on his bike, and he had been taken to the hospital.

At first, we all thought it must have been a minor incident. And then we saw him in the hospital.

He was completely bandaged from head to foot, hooked

up to all kinds of machines, with tubes and wires everywhere. His brain and spine had been damaged. He was unresponsive, in a coma, lying in a bleak hospital room that reeked of medicine. I was in disbelief. We had survived a bloody massacre and traveled to the other side of the world, only to have Dad die in America? He had done everything to get us here, to start a new life for the family and give us a future. I was so devastated, I couldn't think. I thought my heart would crack open. I couldn't imagine my life without my wise, gentle father. Hadn't we been through enough? We talked to him, telling him we loved him, hoping he could hear us.

"Dad, blink if you can understand us," we implored. He didn't blink. Mom had that despairing look on her face like she did after the massacre. She prodded me to talk to him. I didn't know what to say to someone who wasn't responding. He looked dead.

"Hi, Dad," I said, holding his hand. I looked back at Mom, unsure what else to say. She cried and cried.

While my dad lay in a coma, I had to start school. I did not allow myself to think about how my father might never wake up again. I knew that if I let my mind go there, I would not be able to function. I pushed it out of my head. My brain, and my heart, simply could not face it.

My school that year was different from the one I had

attended for those few horrible weeks of sixth grade. This school, Thomas Jefferson High, was another public school, a sprawling brick compound. It was for kids in the seventh through twelfth grades, and the students were mostly immigrants and refugees. Once again, I had no friends there. Still, I knew a little more English this time around. I hoped things might go more smoothly because I had a better sense of what to expect.

But no. Seventh grade started out even worse than the sixth. The kids were more unfriendly. They gave me hostile looks. There was a group of girls who would ask me random questions so they could make fun of the way I spoke when I replied. They would repeat the words I said, mocking my accent and laughing hysterically. They seemed to find this game entertaining. I stopped answering their questions. I started taking English-language classes, hoping that would help. But every day was a fresh hell. I hated school. Other immigrant kids got picked on too, especially Muslim girls who wore modest clothing, such as long skirts and baggy shirts. Any kids who were different became targets.

At the same time, I could sense that the kids around me were hurting in their own way. Many of them seemed angry, unhappy, and poor. They didn't live in the glittery America I had imagined. They wolfed down their food in the cafeteria at lunch, as if they were starving, and I realized they probably had little food at home. But I didn't see why they felt a need to be so mean to me. I went home anxious and upset at the end of each day, but I couldn't talk to my mom about it because she wasn't familiar with my new environment. And she had tremendous problems of her own, working in the grueling factory by day and visiting my dad at night.

We went to the hospital to see him every evening. His condition remained unchanged. We would say a few words to him, then sit there for hours. The doctors never gave us good news. All we heard was: "No changes. No changes." Sometimes church members would stop by and pray. Over the weeks, the doctors began asking my mom if they should pull the plug. His chances of waking up grew slimmer. Mom said no.

At home, my siblings and I had to help Mom figure out the bills because she was busy working and didn't have time to learn English. She needed our help to translate. I was getting better at English. Sometimes it felt like I was the parent, teaching her things.

It was all too much. I grew angry at the world, furious at God. I lost my faith. I decided there was no God and that everything my parents had told me about him was a lie. I thought no one loved us and no one cared, least of all God.

My family was falling apart. People from church would ask, "How are you doing?" I hated that question. How were we doing? We were doing terribly. I listened to people praying to God and thought: You're all fools. God won't help you.

I decided I would never go to church again. I told myself that if my dad died, I would not cry. I would stop feeling anything at all. I was very angry. I hated my life.

School continued to be a minefield, with kids shunning and mocking me, and I dreaded going there every day. There was one girl named Chantelle who tried to talk to me, but she spoke so fast, I could hardly understand her. She was from Tanzania but had managed to assimilate into American culture, as she had been in the States for about three years. She seemed confident and brash. She covered her hair with a head scarf and wore modest skirts, in keeping with her cultural roots, but she spoke English in a way that sounded American. She sounded like the African American kids—in other words, the black kids from America. I was quickly learning that I was not considered African American, even though I was from Africa and I was living in America. My words came out sounding different from theirs. In fact, as I began to learn and speak more English, the African American kids started accusing me of sounding "white." And they did not consider this to be a good thing.

I didn't understand the difference between black and white. Growing up in Congo, being black was not an issue for me. My skin color was something I never thought about. I didn't understand why sounding "white" would be considered bad among black kids, or even what it meant to sound white. No one was teaching me how to speak English one way or the other, "black" or "white." I wondered if I would ever learn to talk the right way. And I wondered what the "right" way was. Seventh grade was the first year when I realized how far from home I had come, and how far I had to go to learn my new world.

I didn't talk about it much with my siblings. We were all trying to work through our own challenges. Everything was new to all of us. I'll never forget Adele's experience with culture shock at a high school track meet. She was set to run in a competition, and then a gun went off to mark the start of the race. No one had told her to expect a gunshot. She thought someone was shooting at people. She ran off the field.

As for me, at least one thing was going my way: My hair was finally growing longer, so I could start braiding it and shed the scratchy wig.

I tried my best to block out the angst—the kids at school, my dad in the hospital—and focus on my studies. I did well in my classes, especially in math and science, which

These are my portraits of survivors
of the Gatumba massacre that were
first shown at the Visual Studies Workshop in
Rochester, New York, in 2012. Included are some
words from the courageous people pictured.

HERITAGE MUNYAKURI is my eldest brother. After surviving year of trauma from being a child soldier, Heritage almost lost his life in Gatumba. He was shot in both of his arms the night of the massacre. Heritage now resides in Rochester, New York, with his wife, Monique, and two beautiful daughters, Joy and Shalom. He is a pastor at New Hope Free Methodist Church.

ESPERANCE SERUHUNGU is studying business administration
in college. "August thirteenth was not like any other. I watched my people getting
shot and burned alive. I lost my mother, my uncles, and my friends. I got shot in
the leg, but that isn't the wound that hurts. What hurts me the most every day of
my life is that Agathon Rwasa and Pasteur Habimana are still walking free. Until
these men—who openly took responsibility for the massacre—are treated as the
criminals they are, I will never heal. I want the international community to show
us that they care about us, that our lives matter by taking action against these men
and a country that shelters criminals."

DESIRE RUSENGO survived the 2004 Gatumba massacre. "I lost my mother and two young brothers Claude and Musore on the night of the attack. I am now a United States citizen living in Virginia. I am a full-time employee of General Dynamics Electric Boat."

G.R.S.F, Inc.

www.gatumbasurvivors.org

FIDELE SEBAHIZI was resettled in California in 2007 following the Gatumba massacre. "During the attack, my brother and his two children were shot but were lucky enough to survive. I urge anyone with influence to fight for marginalized and persecuted communities, such as Banyamulenge. It is important that we stand against anyone who tries to oppress another human being in any form. I recently moved to Texas with my beautiful wife and six-year-old daughter. My goal is to serve the American community as a police officer."

ALINE KAMARIZA was six years old when the massacre happened. "I am lucky to have survived. I lost both of my parents and my uncle. I got shot in the leg and suffered severe burns on most of my body. I am now a senior in high school, working a part-time job and heading to college. I am thankful for my life and how far I have come."

TERIZAYA NYAMASOMO lost her husband and three children in Gatumba. She was resettled in Albany, New York, where she lives with her grandchildren.

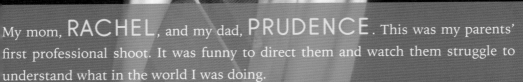

My mom, RACHEL, and my dad, PRUDENCE. This was my parents' first professional shoot. It was funny to direct them and watch them struggle to understand what in the world I was doing.

This is the only surviving photo of my sister Deborah and me, taken in Burundi before the massacre. Pictured from left to right: Dad, Mom, Deborah (front), me, my uncle Rumenge, and Princesse.

Above, left: Mercy High School Show Choir. Above, right: A funny photo before junior prom with my friends Leah (left) and Mackenzie (right). Below: My family at Princesse's college graduation, from left to right: Alex, me, Mom, Princesse, Dad, Adele, and Heritage.

Above: My siblings and me at Alex's high school graduation. Below: At Christmas in 2013 with my cousin Claudine, Adele, and my mom (left to right).

Above, left: My date, CJ, and me dressed up for the senior ball in 2013. Above, right: High school graduation with my mother. Below: We celebrate my sister's wedding in Rwanda with Claudine, Adele, and Princesse.

I reunited with Foroteya (right) in Phoenix, Arizona. My family and Foroteya shared a tent in Gatumba. We recently connected after each had thought for years that the other had died during the massacre.

These photos are from a trip to Rwanda in 2016. This is the boarding school I attended while living there from 2005 to 2006. I wanted to go back and thank the director of this school for giving me an opportunity to learn. This school gave me joy in a time when everything seemed dark. They took me in and gave me a sense of normalcy.

The entrance to College Baptiste De Kabaya.

Above: The girls' dorms. Below: My classroom.

confounded some of the other kids, since my English was still raw. I kept plugging away at the language, and my English-language teacher, Mrs. Khoji, took a personal interest in me. She truly cared about her students and got to know them personally. She saw how hard I worked with my studies, and how I struggled to fit in socially. And then she did something special for me: she helped me apply to a private Catholic girls' school, Our Lady of Mercy, for the eighth grade.

I went to Mercy to take an admissions test. The school was a different world from Jefferson, with a leafy campus straight from a movie: The main building looked like a castle, surrounded by a sprawling lawn of freshly cut grass. The girls wore uniforms and looked confident and content. I was intimidated. As much as I despised Jefferson, at least I was in the same boat as my fellow students, who were mostly poor like me. Still, the prospect of going to Mercy excited me. I had a flash of hope. But I remained angry at the world.

NINETEEN

ALMOST THREE MONTHS AFTER DAD WENT into a coma, I came home from school one afternoon and heard the news: he woke up.

We rushed to the hospital. His eyes were open. His hands were moving. He could nod his head, but he couldn't speak. He was still beat up, and hooked to the machines. His head remained wrapped in bandages. It was hard to look at him in that state, and I was nervous about talking to him. He looked different, distant, haunted. It reminded me of when Heritage came home, all bloody from serving as a child soldier, and I was afraid of him. Mom saw me eyeing my dad shyly.

"Hold his hand," she said. I walked up to him and grabbed his hand, then quickly let it go.

Mom looked so happy that Dad was back with us again. The entire family was overjoyed. We could finally breathe. But my dad looked so vulnerable, it pained me to think that he had finally reached a point where he could help his family, only to end up helpless himself. The doctors warned us that Dad would have gaps in his memory. They advised us to be careful talking to him. They said that instead of telling him a lot of things about the past, we should try to help him remember things on his own.

He remained in the hospital through the winter months, working to regain his memory and physical movement. He gradually began to talk, but he was mixed up about where he was and what had happened. Soon it became clear that he had lost serious chunks of his memory. I grew more comfortable being around him, but wondered if he would ever be the same.

He came home with us to recuperate that spring. At first, he was disoriented, like a ghost of his former self. We had to remind him of so many things. He would misplace items around the house. He would ask us a question and we would answer, and then he would ask the same question thirty minutes later. It was a difficult time. I wanted my strong, invincible dad to come back, the man who dodged gunfire in the massacre and escaped with bullet holes in his shirt collar. But I realized he still was that man: He had survived not only a massacre, but a devastating body blow from a vehicle that had nearly taken his life. He had fought his way out of a three-month coma. He was, indeed, invincible.

We learned that the van had hit him at a crosswalk. He was crossing the street with his bike, when the van hit him and drove away.

Over the weeks, my dad's memory returned, and his personality started to come back too. Being home, surrounded by his loved ones, helped him regain his sense of self. I was curious about what it had been like to be in a coma, and I peppered him with questions.

"Dad, how did it feel when you were in the coma?" I asked. "Were you aware that you were alive?"

"I was aware of my existence, but I did not know where I was," he said. "I didn't know if I was still on earth, or somewhere else."

"Could you hear us talking to you?" I asked.

"No," he said. "I did not hear your voices. But I did have dreams."

He was in the middle of one of those dreams when he

finally awoke, he said. He was dreaming that he was at a church event we call a "crusade," a big prayer gathering.

One of my dad's doctors was from Kenya, and he became a friend to our family. He told us the best markets to find African food, and introduced us to other African families in Rochester. I met an African woman named Mariana who helped me braid my hair. The braids were super-tight and hurt my head, but they looked good. Having the right hair was an important step toward fitting in.

At school, things were looking up. My English-language teacher, Mrs. Khoji, came to my house to tell me that I had received a scholarship to the Catholic school for eighth grade. She said the school had the highest of standards and that I would like it there. I couldn't stop grinning. I said good-bye to my seventh-grade hell.

That summer, I hung around with Mabel and my youth-group friends. Mabel attended a suburban public school, so I didn't get to see much of her during the school year. One day, the youth group invited me along for an overnight party that sounded weird to me—a camping trip. I had never heard of camping. I imagined we would go to the woods and hike and swim, then go to sleep in a bed in a house. When I heard that we would be sleeping on the ground for three days, outside, under a tent, I thought that was insane. People did this on purpose? It sounded like a refugee camp. Goodness, I thought. Are these people so bored, so privileged, that they want to sleep outside on the ground instead of in their comfy beds? I didn't understand why people would want to get bitten by bugs all night when they had a more luxurious option. I wondered if people understood that some people have to live their lives sleeping on the ground in camps.

My friends tried to convince me that camping was fun, a way to escape from stress. If you really want to get away from stress, I thought, why not turn off the phones, read a book, go swimming? Some of the kids had swimming pools in their backyards.

On my first night of camping, I woke up in a bloody sleeping bag. I had gotten my period for the first time. I couldn't believe the timing. Of course my first period would wait to arrive until I was sleeping outside on the ground in the middle of the woods, surrounded by boys. It couldn't have happened the day before? I crept out of the tent, found Mabel, and whispered the news.

"Congratulations!" she said.

"No, this is a nightmare!" I said.

I knew that everyone in the camp would find out within minutes, including the boys—mortifying. I was so embarrassed. I was afraid I would be leaking blood everywhere.

What if no one had any products? And there were two more days to go at the campsite. I knew I would hate camping.

Mabel called a chaperone over, a woman we called Miss Trish. Mabel explained what had happened, and Miss Trish looked a bit taken aback. I was fourteen years old, so maybe she thought I was a late bloomer. She hugged me.

"Oh sweetie, congratulations!" she exclaimed. "You're a woman now."

I wanted to tell her to keep it down. I hadn't given much thought to getting my period, although I knew it would come one day: I had older sisters, after all. But I was always too busy riding bikes and climbing trees to think about it.

We were supposed to go swimming that day at the camp, and I worried that I would turn the lake red. Miss Trish went around asking girls if they had any products for me, until finally she found some. She kept smiling and congratulating me, her voice booming. We had to wash my pajamas and sleeping bag in the lake. Sure enough, all the boys knew my secret. But they looked as embarrassed as I did.

By the time I started eighth grade, I had developed boobs and hips, and I started wearing bras. I thought, okay, that's one thing I've got going for me. My sisters made fun of me— even more so when they saw how embarrassed it made me. The tomboy in the family was growing up.

TWENTY

IN EIGHTH GRADE, I ENTERED A DIFFERENT world. My new school, Our Lady of Mercy, was a polite and proper private Catholic school, with girls in plaid skirts and navy polo shirts. The halls were orderly, not filled with chaos like my last school. At this point, I could hold my own speaking English. The kids seemed friendly. They were mostly white. They did not seem openly hostile toward me, like some of the kids at my last school, although I could see certain girls sizing me up, judging me. At Mercy, I began to understand a lot of things about America—and about being black in America.

I made three new friends quickly: Leah, Mackenzie, and

Shantavia. Leah and Mackenzie were white, both shy. Mackenzie looked like a Disney princess: She was petite and sweet; she looked like someone who would walk around with a halo of cheerful birds singing over her head. Shantavia was black and super-smart, a bit nerdy. They were kind to me, and patient. When they discussed things like American TV shows and pop culture, I would have no idea what they were talking about. I hadn't grown up watching American shows, and I didn't get the references. I tried to catch up by watching plenty of TV, but I had a long way to go. There were so many cultural disconnects, but my friends accepted me. They hadn't really hung around one another until I came along, and we became our own little group.

Things got a little weird once we started eating lunch together. That's because the black girls generally sat together in the cafeteria. They had white friends, but at lunchtime, the black girls all hung out together, sitting in their own group. I could sense that they felt I should be sitting with them, but also, they knew I didn't really belong. I didn't belong with the white kids either. I could feel that mysterious divide between black and white again, just like at my last school, and I didn't understand the reason for it. In the cafeteria, my friends and I sat at the end of the table where the black girls sat. Shantavia was friends with the black girls but sat with us; she had always done her own thing. Gradually, I got to know the black girls from sitting at that table.

The black girls spoke with an urban lingo I did not know, and they sometimes said I sounded "white," just like the kids at my last school had said. When they said this to me, I would say, "What do you mean?" It was frustrating. I started to think: Am I not being a good black person? I really wanted to fit in with them. I wanted to be black and to make black friends—I wanted to be friends with people who looked like me. I wondered if they assumed I was from a wealthy white district because of the way I spoke. Of course, that could not have been further from the truth. Eventually, I started trying to sound "black" when I talked to them. I'm sure I sounded ridiculous. It's amazing that they didn't laugh me out of the school. Still, I kept trying. It got to a point that I would switch the way I spoke, depending on whether I was talking to someone black or white, except among my good friends. I was hardly even aware that I was speaking differently to different people. I was trying to belong in both groups, but I belonged in neither. I looked black, but I sounded white.

I also noticed that the white and black kids talked about different topics, and read different books: The black girls read popular black teen novels; the white girls read *Harry Potter*.

I realized that race was a very big deal in America. There

were so many expectations about how I was supposed to act, who I was supposed to be. I couldn't figure out my identity. No one said, "Here's your manual. Here's how to be black." I was not well versed in American history, but I had learned the basics in school in Africa. I knew things like the names of presidents and states. I knew that slavery had happened, but I didn't know all the details. I couldn't say how many times Martin Luther King Jr. had been arrested. It wasn't part of my history.

And the American kids knew nothing of my history in Africa. Some of them seemed to assume I had grown up in a jungle. One day, a girl asked, "Sandra, were you surprised when you saw shoes for the first time in America?" I was so offended and embarrassed, I cried. As if I had never seen a pair of shoes until I came to America! One of my teachers, Mr. Desain, overheard the conversation and told the girl her remark was inappropriate, and she had to apologize.

The girl's comment was not unusual. Kids often asked me things like that. I would be sitting in the lunchroom and someone would ask, "What did you wear in Africa?" Guess what: We wore clothes! We drove around in cars! And planes go there too! Sometimes I would have a little fun with my answers, saying, "We wore grass skirts and bras made of leaves. We go from place to place by swinging around on vines like Tarzan. I had a pet lion and a pet elephant, and they lived together in a mud hut. My parents were so wealthy, my siblings and I each had our own individual mud huts, if you can believe it. Oh, and I had a monkey that talked!"

Sometimes the kids would ask if I believed in God, and they seemed dubious when I said yes, as if there were no religions in Africa.

I suppose it's not so surprising that the kids thought people from Africa were from Mars. The images of Africa on American TV were all the same: There were the ads for charity groups showing a white lady holding a starving black child, flies landing all over the kid. Indeed, Africans might be poor, but we know how to swat flies. Then there were the features focusing on some remote and obscure rural tribe. And if Africa ever made the evening news, it was because of a disease outbreak. The news reports made it seem like we were people from a different planet, people from "over there." We are all human beings. Yes, Africa has many problems, but there is so much beauty, so much goodness too. In America, the images of Africa make it seem as if it is a place where only bad things happen. Conversely, in Africa, the images of America make it seem like it is a land so divine, only good things happen.

My teachers at Mercy didn't treat me any differently

than the other students, and I appreciated that. They knew I was a refugee, but didn't know the details of my past. They assumed I was intelligent. They didn't talk down to me. But sometimes, I wished they wouldn't call on me in class. I did not like to speak in class like I did back home, when I was the confident star student. In America, I was embarrassed about my accent, and worried I wouldn't find the right words in English. I dreaded getting called on to answer questions. I would sit there silently, sweating. But my teachers pushed me hard, and now I can see that this was a good thing.

One day in history class, my teacher talked about America's history of slavery. During the lesson, the white kids glanced around at the black kids; there were just a few of us in the class. I think the white kids were curious, or perhaps they were afraid that we would be offended by the topic. I didn't know how to react when they looked at me. I wanted to say, "Why are you looking at me?" It seemed as if they assumed that as a black person, I was a speaker for all black people. But I was learning the history of American slavery myself. At the same time, I didn't want to come off as clueless. I didn't want the black kids to say, "She doesn't know how to be black." I worried that I would never be black enough.

And then, something unexpected happened in history

class, and my classmates had an opportunity to understand something about me. We watched *Hotel Rwanda*, the movie about the bloody genocide in Rwanda that left as many as a million people dead. My teacher, who knew a little about my past, had warned me beforehand that the film would be difficult to watch, but I wanted to see it. As I began to watch it, however, I became so emotional, I had to leave the class. The movie brought me back to the atrocious conflicts I had witnessed in my own life, and I needed some air. I walked the hallways, went to my locker, and then returned to class later.

"Is everything okay?" my teacher asked me.

"It's a little too close to home," I said.

The kids in my class were shaken by the movie too. You could see it on their faces. They asked, "How could something like this happen?" I'm glad my teacher showed us the film. It's important for schools to expose kids to difficult topics like that, to help them understand what's going on in the rest of the world. I realized that my classmates cared when they saw the images of human rights abuses and war. They just hadn't been tuned in to what was happening.

Since I was the only one who could speak to war in Africa, I shared a little of my story with the students for the first time. The kids were blown away. They had no idea what I had been through. I'm not even sure if they really believed me.

"No way," they said.

But I think, on some level, we came to an understanding that day.

TWENTY-ONE

OVER THE WEEKS, AS I LEARNED MORE ABOUT American history, I started to understand more about what it meant to be African American, and the ongoing and complex fight for equality. But I was still very confused. I noticed that on TV it seemed as if black people were always committing crimes. In fact, it seemed like black people were solely responsible for crime in America. On news shows and on fictional shows alike, it was a constant parade of black people getting arrested and thrown in jail. The images were so negative, I was sort of scared of being black. Those images did not represent me, or the black girls I was meeting at school. I wondered if black people in America were mostly bad.

I thought that perhaps I needed to prove to white people that I wasn't like the criminals I saw on TV. It made me question so many things.

I started doing my own research and talking to the African American girls at school, engaging in conversations with them at lunch. The black girls were on top of any news stories involving race and discrimination, such as controversial police shootings, and they also discussed the kinds of everyday hurdles that black people face in America. I was impressed by their knowledge. There were three girls in particular who always had insightful things to say: Taryn, Sadaris, and Tae'lor. My white friends, Leah and Mackenzie, listened intently to the discussions. They were such good listeners. They were learning with me. I began to gain a deeper understanding of the complexities of race in America. I learned that the way black people were portrayed on TV certainly did not reflect the much more nuanced and complicated reality. I learned about tensions between black people and the police. I learned how black parents would warn their kids to be careful around the officers, because a black kid could get shot for simply running down the street. I learned how black parents would advise their kids to keep their driver's license somewhere accessible, so they wouldn't have to dig deep for it, lest the cops think they were reaching for a gun.

I also noticed that the white girls in school seemed afraid of the black girls, worried that they would get beaten up if they crossed them. But the black girls were the sweetest, smartest, nerdiest kids. They could never beat anyone up. Still, there was that perception that they were scary or dangerous.

And one day, I had my own experience of being perceived as "bad" simply because I was black. I was shopping in a Banana Republic at the mall with my friend Leah, and a clerk was following us around the store, keeping an eye on us.

Finally, the clerk told us, "There's nothing here for you."

"Okay," I said, and we left, embarrassed and confused.

Perhaps the clerk thought we had no money because we were teenagers. But I had seen other teens in the store, and they hadn't been asked to leave. Outside the store, Leah, who is white, was fuming.

"You realize what just happened, right? She thinks you're going to shoplift because you're black," she said.

That thought hadn't even occurred to me.

"What do you mean?" I asked. I was dressed nicely, as always. I looked like a teen girl. I did not look like a criminal. But I was black. I'll never forget that moment. And incidentally, that store clerk totally blew it—Leah's dad had given her money for the shopping trip. We were ready to spend it.

On that day, I realized it didn't matter how I saw myself,

because other people saw my skin color. Before I came to America, I was Sandra. I was a student, a daughter, a sister. I was African, Congolese. Did I ever define myself as black? No. My skin color didn't determine who I was as a person. Everyone was black. My interests, my beliefs, defined me. My skin color was simply a fact about me, like the fact that I like candy. If you ask who I am as a person, I wouldn't say, "I like candy." That's not a fundamental thing that describes me. But in America, my skin color did define me, at least in other people's eyes. I was black. I was black first, and then I was Sandra.

I had grown up in a war zone, but life in America, I realized, was a different kind of war zone.

I began talking to my parents about what I was learning from my African American friends at school. Mom and Dad had seen all the negative portrayals of black people on TV. They didn't know what to think. They weren't meeting a lot of different people like I was. They were working hard, dealing with their issues.

Mom continued to be the breadwinner, working in the factory while my dad recuperated from his injuries. It was still hard for me to accept the fact that my larger-than-life parents seemed so small in America, so under the radar. Mom took a second job cleaning a movie theater, and I helped her on the weekends.

The movie theater was awful. I could not understand why people would buy giant buckets of popcorn, only to dump them on the floor. We had to clean the theater overnight, after the last show, so the place would be ready for moviegoers the next day. I would go to the theater around ten thirty at night with Mom and my cousin Claudine. We would wait for the last show to end—usually around midnight—and then sweep and mop the floors and scour the bathrooms. People left the toilets in such a mess. They never stopped to think about the fact that someone else had to clean up after them—the unseen people like us at night. It took hours to clean that grimy theater, as there were several screening rooms, and we would generally finish around six in the morning. If there had been a big premiere the night before with a lot of people attending and throwing things on the floor, we would be there until eight in the morning.

My mom did this several nights a week, from Sunday to Thursday—after working all day at the factory. It was a physically demanding job, reaching under the seats in the theater to scrape up goo, scrubbing toilets in the bathroom. By the end of the night, I often felt like my body would give out. But Mom would do that backbreaking job and then go straight to work at the factory the next morning. She did all of this without complaining. She did her work with such grace and resilience, never a gripe. Watching her inspired me to do well in school so I could help her financially one day and she wouldn't have to work so hard.

But I had my bratty moments too. I still had to help my parents translate the bills and other documents at home, which got on my nerves. One time I tried to explain a cable TV bill to my mom when she thought she had been overcharged. She was impatient.

"Call them. Tell them they're charging too much," she said.

I called the cable company, and someone there explained the bill. It turned out we were not being overcharged. I tried to explain it to Mom, but she wasn't buying it.

"Why are you being so nice to them?" she asked. "This is money!"

Then she got on the phone and spoke in broken English, saying, "I no pay! I no pay!"

I wanted no part of that.

Sometimes I would have to make phone calls pretending to be my mom. I would call the home insurers, the credit-card companies. If someone asked me something that I didn't know, I would have to say, "Hold on a second," and then I would ask Mom for the information. I always had to know my parents' passwords for email and other accounts, in case of any problems.

I'm sure it pained my parents to have to ask their kids for help. It must have been hard for them, but I didn't realize that at the time. Back home in Congo, my parents understood everything, and they taught me. Now it was the other way around. I taught them. Every time they asked me to translate a bill, I'd groan about it.

I hated the fact that I couldn't be a normal kid, like the kids around me. Their parents were in charge, and they understood how things worked. My friends' parents drove them everywhere, while my own family didn't have a car. My friends got allowances from their parents, a concept I had never heard of. I was leading a double life, trying to be an American kid at school but coming home to teach my parents English and help them pay the bills. Kids aren't supposed to teach their parents. Essentially, everything my parents knew about American culture came from me. But I still knew so little myself.

Adding to the cultural divide, my fellow students were pretty well off. They'd say things like, "I need to get good grades or I won't get a car for my sixteenth birthday." Really? Your own new car, for your birthday? I didn't even have a cell phone, which of course made me the biggest dork around.

Dad tried to do everything he could to help Mom and the rest of us around the house, like getting up early each day to make breakfast for everyone. That would ordinarily be considered "women's work" in my culture, and some men would never do it, no matter the circumstances. They would expect the woman to do everything. My dad is different from so many men in my culture. Sometimes he would tell us how his property would be divided among all of his kids if he passed away, not just given to the boys, per the tradition. Another example of his awesome feminism.

But I would soon test his limits.

TWENTY-TWO

AS I TRIED TO ASSIMILATE INTO AMERICAN culture, tensions between my parents and me grew. Clothes were one issue. My parents didn't want me wearing short-shorts, which was fine with me—I didn't want my butt hanging out of a tiny pair of shorts—but my friends would come to the house wearing them, and Mom couldn't help but comment. She was good-natured about it; she understood that American culture was different from ours, but still, my friends would come over and she would shake her head. Dad would never say anything, but Mom would say, "Leah, no, no, no," and point at her legs. Or she would pull Mackenzie's shirt down over her shorts to try to cover more of her legs. I would say, "Mom, cut it out!"

I told my friends that my mom said these things out of love. "She might not love your outfit, but she loves you," I said.

Luckily, my friends had a sense of humor about it. They came to expect that when they showed up at my house, my mom would tsk-tsk their outfits. Sometimes they would dress more modestly, like in a knee-length skirt, and say proudly to my mom, "Look!" She would nod approvingly, and they would giggle.

One day I tried to wear a little sundress to church. I walked out of the house, smiling and feeling all cute. Dad just gave me this look. I guess I was showing too much leg. He didn't have to say anything.

"Fine," I said. "I'm not going."

"Good," he said.

I stayed home.

I wanted to be like my American friends. They went on dates with boys, which my parents did not want me to do. My friends' parents actually drove them on dates and dropped them off at the movie theater or a café, because the kids weren't old enough to drive. In Africa, we didn't casually date the way teenagers do in America. If a young couple had a relationship in Congo, there was an end goal—marriage. You didn't just date someone for the heck of it.

One day my mom and I talked about dating. She told me, "Your friends in America do this because it's their culture. It doesn't mean you have to do it." She wanted me to stay within our cultural lanes. Ideally, she wanted me to marry someone from our culture one day too.

"Mom, I'm going to marry a white man," I prodded her. "And what are you going to do about it?"

"Over my dead body," she said. "Sandra, you won't do it. You know you won't. You need to have a traditional wedding."

It's not that Mom had anything against white people; she just thought our cultures were too far apart. For one thing, she thought white people had small, subdued weddings, not major celebrations like in our tribe. She got that idea from an American woman my brother Heritage had dated. The woman was white, and she wanted a small wedding at an inn. The relationship caused a lot of anxiety for my mom, and she and Heritage clashed over it many times. Heritage was the first among her kids to date outside the culture. He was an adult, and there was nothing my mother could do about it. Still, Mom was always nice to the woman. She tried her best to deal with the situation. I'm sure she was relieved when they broke up.

I kept pushing her. "Mom, my best friends are white, and you love them," I said.

"Your friends are your friends—you're not marrying them," she said. "I love your friends, but you're not going to spend the rest of your life with them."

Still, I didn't argue with my parents too much about dating in high school. I had to pick my battles. I had to talk them into so many things, like going to friends' parties. In Congo, teens did not throw their own parties. We would go to parties held by relatives, not by other kids. Everything I was experiencing in my social life in America was new to Mom and Dad. It all had to be negotiated.

My parents and I were growing in different directions. Of course, most teens feel misunderstood. But I considered myself to be genuinely misunderstood because my parents and I were not having the same life experiences: They had not grown up in America. They had not gone to an American high school. They could not guide me.

Things that are the norm in the States, like tampons, were new to my mom. Women wore pads back home. When Adele realized I was wearing tampons, she worried that they took your virginity. It's a common belief in different cultures. When I wanted to wear a bikini to the beach, Mom was appalled by the concept. "You're going to show that much skin?" she asked. Eventually, I wore the bikini.

We had some major negotiations over a formal dance at school. I tried to convince my parents that I needed an expensive dress—two hundred dollars—to wear to the event. My siblings were sitting there listening to this request, laughing. In addition to the dress, I would be asking a boy to the dance. I went to a school for girls, so I would have to ask a boy. My parents were taken aback. A dance? A dress? A date?

"You want to spend that much money on a dress for one night?" Mom asked. "Would you ever wear it again?"

"If you want to dance, why don't you dance right here?" Dad said. "We have plenty of space in the living room."

Mom thought that was a good idea. "Yes," she said. "Why don't your friends come here? They could sleep here."

"Where would they sleep?" I asked.

"In your bed," Dad said.

I rolled my eyes. I'd had sleepovers with Leah and Mackenzie, but I would not be hosting a school dance in my living room. My brothers would be messing with us all night. They always got involved with my slumber parties, getting my friends to play African card games, teaching them dance moves and then laughing at them. It was actually kind of fun, and my friends embraced it. But a dance in the living room? No.

My parents agreed to think about it. They didn't want me to be excluded. They had to choose their battles just like I chose mine.

Over the next few days, I tried to get more strategic in my tactics. Instead of saying, "Mackenzie's mother lets her go to dances," in which case my mom would say, "You are not Mackenzie," I would say, "It's normal for kids to go to dances." I would continue, "You don't want me to be a social outcast, right? You don't want to look at me sitting here, with no social life and no friends, until the end of time, right?"

My mom, ever the comedian, would say, "Yes, I like looking at you."

My siblings found all of this hilarious. Secretly, I'm sure they were cheering me on. I was the one fighting most of the battles since they were all much older, except for Alex, who had his own negotiations to navigate, usually involving staying out late with friends.

My parents managed to come to terms with me on the school dance. I went with my friend Michael from my church youth group. His dad drove him over to my house before the dance, and Michael awkwardly handed me my corsage. Mom did buy me a nice dress, blue with a sweetheart neckline.

I know how much I pushed my parents. For me to tell my dad, "I'm going out with a boy, and I won't be back until after midnight," and for my dad to say yes, that's huge. I was taking steps, but they were taking leaps. It was a real diplomacy act. They had their traditions and values, and I was growing up in a different world, a different culture. I had to try not to get too far ahead of them, and they had to try to catch up with me. Even though I didn't fully realize it at the time, my parents were good sports about all of this. And they were smart too. They knew that the tighter parents hold on to their kids, the more the kids want to break away.

I wish the resettlement system for refugees could help mentor parents—not to tell them how to raise their kids, but to help them understand the new culture their children are experiencing. Parents have to learn how to raise their kids in a foreign land. Kids need guidance from their parents, but their parents have no idea what influences their children are facing in their new world. In my experience, the schools never called my parents to discuss me, probably because of the language barrier. My parents were on their own.

I also wish the resettlement program offered counseling for refugees. They are survivors of trauma. Moving them from here to there isn't enough. We have to care about the people, and help them deal with their past. How can they become a part of a new society when they have never dealt with the terrors of their past? People sometimes say to me,

"Oh, you're so lucky." When people say that, I kind of want to punch them in the face. Just because you resettle people doesn't mean their lives are suddenly perfect. I lost my little sister in a massacre, fell into the depths of poverty, and fled my homeland. All that, to get to America.

TWENTY-THREE

AS MORE SURVIVORS OF OUR MASSACRE
made their way to America, we began to connect with one
another on Facebook, as we were all scattered across the
country. And we decided to meet up once a year for a reunion,
on the anniversary of the attack in August. We would meet
in different states around the country each year, reconnect,
and remember.

We elected members of our community to organize the
events. I'll never forget my first reunion, in St. Louis, Mis-
souri. I saw so many familiar faces, including two of my best
friends from the refugee camp, Inge and Desire. I had sat
with Inge on the morning after the massacre, paralyzed by

the bloody scene before us. He had managed to resettle in Virginia with his uncle. When we saw each other, we hugged, hard, and I cried, my tears wetting his shirt. We didn't say much. We didn't need words. We each knew what the other was feeling. I couldn't believe my old friend from that devastating day was right there in front of me. Memories of that nightmarish morning came crashing back.

The gathering was intense. There was not a lot of talking, but a lot of crying. We hugged and held each other close. We sang the old gospel songs of our people. Every time I saw people's faces, it took me back to the last time I had seen them in the camp. I saw a girl named Kama from my tent. She had lost her parents and brother in the massacre. This was the first time I had seen her since that night. Now living with her grandmother in America, she had been badly burned in the attack, the scars stretching across one side of her body. She used to play with my sister Deborah. I thought about how random it was that we had survived when so many others had not. The people who you thought would survive—the teenage boys, the able-bodied people—didn't necessarily make it. But young girls like us did. I will never know why.

At one point, we all watched footage of the morning after the attack. There had been some reporters with cameras there early that morning, interviewing officials. The vice president of Congo spoke, as did the president of Burundi. We saw images of dead bodies and limbs strewn across the camp. The grounds were still smoking from the fire. It was the first time I had seen the footage, and it brought me back. I cried, and Inge reached over and held my hand. I could tell he was trying not to cry himself. People around us were sobbing, but we were all together, bonded for life, and there was comfort in that. We had all been through the same ordeal together. No one was there saying, "I'm sorry for your loss."

But I still had not faced my past. I was trying so hard to navigate my conflicting worlds at school and at home, I left it buried in the back of my mind.

I did have one escape from this constant internal struggle: a church choir that my dad started, like the one he had formed in Rwanda. I was less furious at God these days, thanks to Dad's recovery. My siblings and I began singing at local churches. Over time, we taught the American kids in church to sing with us as well. We spent hours teaching them how to sing in Swahili. We would teach them how to pronounce different words, like *upendo*, which means "love." Many of the songs were about God's love. Some words in Swahili have a silent "n," which was always a pronunciation challenge. When my friends goofed up with the language, it made me laugh. "This is how I feel when I mess up in English!" I said.

When we performed with the American kids, audiences were wowed. I loved singing. It was freeing. We raised some money from our performances and sent it back to the kids from our tribe in Africa. We called our group the Foundation of Hope Ministries.

Our choir began singing at churches around the Northeast. My sister Princesse would give an introduction to the performance, describing our history. One night, when we were getting ready to sing at a church in Pennsylvania, Princesse didn't feel well. The mother of one of the kids asked me to give the introduction. "You're the next most fluent," she said.

Oh no! I thought. I couldn't imagine standing up and speaking in English to an audience of adults. But I didn't have a lot of time to think about it. Someone had to do it, and I found myself agreeing. I had a copy of the speech, and I figured I could read the words Princesse had written. I stood up in front of everyone and began to speak, my voice trembling. I was self-conscious about my accent and my English, worried that I would bungle the words.

"My name is Sandra Uwiringiyimana. My family and I are from the Democratic Republic of the Congo," I began. I read the first part of the speech, explaining the history of the Banyamulenge people. I got to the part about the Gatumba massacre, and I paused. My eyes blurred with tears, and I searched the audience for help from my siblings, but none came. I could barely read the words on the page, and they didn't feel right to me. I stopped for a moment and caught my breath. I looked up and started speaking from memory. I had never thought about what I would say to an audience, so I was unsure if anything I was saying made sense. I simply spoke from the heart. For the first time, I let it all out. Raw memories tumbled forth about my war-ridden childhood and the brutal refugee camp. I described how we searched for Deborah's body on the morning after the massacre. I moved forward to our life in Rwanda after the attack, when it was a quest to find drinking water. I looked out at the congregation, and everyone was crying, including my mom.

I could see that my words stunned people. They looked angry, too, as they learned what we had endured. It made me feel angry as well. I wish I could have told the congregation that my experience was unique, an isolated event. But it wasn't. Millions of people have been uprooted and displaced by war. In fact, I was shocked that the audience was shocked. I had grown up in a land where war was so common, we basically sighed and said, "Oh man, this again?" Any given day, you could be on the run. There, it would have been unusual to go for an entire school year without being interrupted by war.

At the same time, as I watched the people in the church cry, I had a realization: They cared. I had assumed that people in America did not care. But in that instant, I realized they did. They just didn't know our story. They didn't know what life was like in a refugee camp, or how it felt to endure a massacre. In America, we live in a world where Kim Kardashian dominates the news, not massacres in Africa.

My perspective shifted on that night. Suddenly, I wanted people to know. I wanted people to know about Deborah, about how her life was taken. I wanted Americans to know that my people were not some kind of strange beings "over there," but people like them—people with hobbies and dreams and talents.

I gave more talks at our performances, sometimes with Princesse, sometimes on my own. The more I talked, the more I cried. I was exhausted after each talk, and would fall asleep in the car on the way home from the performance. But I liked letting people know what we had been through, describing the plight of refugees. Perhaps I was helping foster understanding between cultures, in some small way.

Still, I carried tremendous anger about the massacre and about how Deborah had been taken from me. Our choir group preached forgiveness, but I did not forgive. I could not let my anger go. I thought that the burning pain in my chest was Deborah. And I needed to hold on to that pain, in order to hold on to Deborah. If I let that pain and anger go, I would be letting her go. I would be letting her down, letting all of my people down. And so I held on to it. I held on to the pain. I held on for her.

In time, some of that anger began to fade, or rather, to shift. It happened gradually, as I kept singing and talking to people at churches. I thought about how so many of the killers at the massacre in Gatumba were teenagers—kids who had been taught to hate us, but did not know why they hated us. I thought about how the parents of the killers were the ones who had taught the kids to hate. This all started because someone hated someone. And so I stopped feeling so angry at the killers. Of course, I wanted the perpetrators to be held responsible, and if I saw Deborah's killers standing in front of me today, I don't know if I could forgive them. But I tried to take a broader view: The people who shot the bullets were part of a cycle of hate that they had been taught since they were born. Hate killed my sister, and I didn't want to be part of that cycle.

I started thinking about Deborah differently too. I had been focusing on the horrid few seconds when the bullets took her life, but she had lived six years before that. I thought about those years and the times I had with her that I cherished. It was such a short time to know and to love someone, but it was six years of good memories, versus a few seconds of tragedy.

I was more determined than ever to keep Deborah's memory alive. Sometimes, my mom would introduce me to people as the youngest child, and it bothered me deeply. Deborah was the youngest. I wanted everyone to know.

I would correct Mom, saying, "I'm the second youngest. We lost my little sister."

Mom would sigh and say yes. I'm sure she was exhausted by having to explain it all the time. But I wanted to explain it every single time. And I still couldn't shake that inexplicable feeling that Deborah would come back one day. I think because we had never been able to have a funeral, to visit her grave, to mourn her properly, it never became real to me.

"You can't escape death, no matter how young or old you are," Mom told me. "When it's your day, it's your day."

I tried to accept that. But Deborah's day came far too soon.

TWENTY-FOUR

IN MY JUNIOR YEAR OF HIGH SCHOOL, THE annual reunion of my people was held in nearby Syracuse, New York, and my brother Alex and I started a project that would change the course of my life. I was still on my campaign with the choir to help people understand our experience, and a friend at church named Joanna suggested that I take portraits of my people and interview them about their experiences. She said a local gallery in Rochester, called the Visual Studies Workshop, had been showing photography from genocides around the world, and perhaps we could do an exhibit there. I loved the idea, even though the gallery seemed like a pipe dream. Joanna lent me her camera, and I took it to the reunion.

Taking portraits of my people was such a moving experience, I felt as if my heart began to heal. It was so touching that people would share their thoughts and memories with me. Their trust meant everything. For the pictures, we had a simple white screen for a backdrop, and people could sit or stand for their portrait, whatever made them feel comfortable. Many chose to sit. I took most of the photos, while Alex worked on perfecting the lighting, with some help from Joanna. We were learning; we barely knew what we were doing. We didn't expect anything major to come from it. We saw it as an adventure. Joanna was advising us, coaching us on how to find good angles.

In the portraits, I wanted to show that my people had not been defeated. I aimed to show their energy, their life. I took a picture of Kama, the girl who had been burned as a child in the attack. No one thought she would survive her injuries, but here she was, a young woman now with such strength. My friend Desire sat for me too. Seeing him sitting there, smiling, made me smile too. He asked if he should smile for the photo or not, and I said to do whatever he felt. We were all family, taking family portraits. I recorded videos of people sharing their memories as well. My mom talked about how it felt to flee for her life.

"We were born into wars," Mom said. "We grew up fleeing from place to place, and our fathers and our mothers carried us on their backs. We also started fleeing with our own children on our backs, because every year, we expected persecution."

Afterward, Joanna helped guide Alex and me through the process of putting together an exhibit. I decided on the size of the portraits, the frames—every little detail. To my amazement, the gallery accepted the exhibit—twenty-two portraits of my people, accompanied by write-ups and videos about their lives. Alex and I did a video of ourselves as well, describing why we had decided to do the project, and how I wanted to show the resilience and dignity of my people. It made me think about who I was, and about what I wanted to do. For the first time, I felt strongly that I wanted to be an activist, a voice for the displaced. This is who I need to be, I told myself.

On opening night, my entire family arrived. The portraits came to life. The pictures looked poignant and powerful, looming large on the walls. My parents were impressed. They watched as people came up to me and asked me questions about the exhibit.

"Who are all these people?" Mom asked, looking around at the attendees.

People from the local art community had come, along with classmates and friends. The following week, I gave talks at the gallery for high school students and refugee kids. They had a slew of questions, and it felt good to be able to talk with young people about my experience. I could tell they were truly interested. They walked around and studied the pictures and read all the quotes from my people. They asked about individuals, and about how they were related or connected. I found it energizing, talking to kids. They wanted to know about people, not about war.

Around this time, a producer for a big women's conference in New York City, the Women in the World Summit, learned about the exhibit and reached out to me through the gallery. I hadn't heard of the summit, but when I Googled it, I saw that it was run by a famous magazine editor, Tina Brown. I saw that Hillary Clinton, Angelina Jolie, and activists from all over the world participated in these summits. I connected with the producer, Mark Young, and he invited me to speak on a panel at the summit, which would be held at Lincoln Center. He said it in such a chill way, like it was nothing special, but I thought: What? Lincoln Center was home to world-famous operas and ballets.

I tried to tell my mom about it, but I was so excited, I could barely get the words out. I was jumping up and down in the living room. When I get wound up, I speak fast, using a jumbled mix of English and Kinyamulenge. Mom, who was busy cleaning the house at the time, looked at me like I was nuts.

"Why don't you stop jumping around and tell me what's going on," she said. "Sit down quietly and explain it to me. I can't understand you."

"Somebody in New York saw my exhibit," I said. "There's a summit. It's huge, Mom. The Women in the World Summit. They invited me!"

Princesse was there and started Googling. When she read about the summit, she said, "Wow!"

I was still hopping up and down.

"You're crazy," Mom said. "You're so American." Mom was not one to get overly excited about things. She came and looked at the computer screen.

"What are they going to do for you?" she asked. To my mom, the most important thing was always education. She thought everything else was a distraction.

"Mom, it's an opportunity," I said. "More people will learn about us and the Banyamulenge people."

Dad wandered in, and I told him the news. He got it.

"It's a platform to help educate people," he said, low-key as always.

Then he sat me down and said, "You need to think about this. Think about what you want to say. This is important."

Soon after, the producer said I would be appearing on a panel with Angelina Jolie and Madeleine Albright, the former secretary of state, talking about war. I couldn't imagine it. Me, onstage with Angelina and the former secretary of state? And this had sprung from our photo exhibit at a little gallery in Rochester? I told my parents, explaining to them who Angelina Jolie and Madeleine Albright were. They were impressed. I also learned that a journalist would be interviewing me for a profile on the *Daily Beast*, scheduled to run at the time of the summit. I spoke with the writer Abigail Pesta for the story, telling her about my past. Then I headed to Lincoln Center with Princesse for a rehearsal the day before the event. The rest of my family would watch the event live-streamed online.

In New York City, the head producer of the summit, Kyle Gibson, took me onstage, and I looked around at the enormous theater.

"How many people will be here?" I asked. It looked like thousands of seats.

"It will be filled up to the top—to the balcony!" Kyle said.

I was nervous. I couldn't eat anything. I kept pacing around. Princesse tried to calm me.

"Just remember, people have never heard this story. They will be hanging on your every word," she said. "People are here because they want to hear your story."

On the day of the event, the plan changed again. The producers said that I would not be speaking on the panel. Instead, I would be doing a one-on-one interview with talk show host Charlie Rose about my experience growing up in a conflict zone.

"I don't know if I can do this," I said to Princesse.

It's a good thing that I didn't have much time to think about it. That night, I walked onstage, my heart thumping. I tried to keep my emotions under control. I have a little trick that I do when I'm nervous: I hold my fingers in my palm, concentrating on their movement, rather than on my nerves. It helps keep me centered.

The lights came up and I sat across from Charlie Rose onstage. Stay calm, I told myself. My insides were in knots.

"You're wise beyond your age," Charlie said. "I think you're still a teenager. What is it that's important, that you know better than anybody in this room?"

As I gathered my thoughts, a summit worker scurried onstage and handed Charlie a bottle of water. He chuckled and apologized for the disruption, saying he had a cold. I loosened up a bit.

"Well, I know that hatred doesn't solve a thing," I said. "I know that justice needs to be fought for. It needs to be demanded. I know that it can come from anyone, even from a teenager like myself."

The audience clapped. Princesse was right: They wanted to hear my story.

My portraits flashed on a big screen overhead. Charlie asked me about the people in the pictures, and I described a little girl in a green dress named Evony. "She's adorable," I said, and Charlie agreed. The audience laughed. "She currently lives in Albany, New York. When I see her, I see a little girl who can't speak for herself. When I look at her, it reminds me that I need to go out there and share the story for little girls like Evony who can't tell it, or who have seen things that no little girl should ever have to experience." The audience clapped again. "She just makes me want to fight for justice, so that no little girl or little boy, or anyone that age—or anyone, for that matter—would have to experience this."

I powered my way through it. I don't know how. I was so relieved when I finished, I barely even heard what Charlie was saying when he asked me a final question: Would I like to introduce the next speaker—Angelina Jolie—to the audience?

No one had told me I would be introducing Angelina!

"Sure?" I said.

And then I was doing it, introducing Angelina to a crowd of thousands. She came to the stage, looking beautiful in a white silk blazer. I thanked her for her work on behalf of refugees, saying she had really helped people like me. She hugged me, and I could see that she was crying. "Thank you, Sandra," she said.

I made my way backstage, thinking: Did that just happen? My sister Princesse embraced me, as did the producers and Charlie Rose. He gave me his card, saying to stay in touch. Princesse told me that Angelina had been crying backstage while she listened to my life story.

A friend of mine started a Twitter account for me that night. People began tweeting at me. The next night, I attended an event related to the summit, the DVF Awards, hosted by fashion designer and women's rights advocate Diane von Furstenberg. She's a big deal, but I had never heard of her until that evening. The event was held at the United Nations. I had to go alone because we ran out of time to get the necessary security clearance for Princesse. I made my way through the security line and the winding halls of the UN compound, until I reached a corner room where the event would be held. There was a table of place cards at the entrance, and I found my name. I noticed a place card for Oprah Winfrey.

"Oh my God," I said to the woman sitting at the table. "Is that *the* Oprah Winfrey?"

"Yup, that's the one!" she said.

I walked into the room, which had been converted from an office space into a fabulous nightclub for the evening, with pink spotlights, zebra-print sofas, palm trees, cocktails, and a delicious Indian buffet. Diane von Furstenberg was honoring powerful women at the event, including Oprah. I was standing there, taking in the scene, when Oprah walked in, glowing in a long green dress, surrounded by an entourage. Some girls were trying to take selfies, maneuvering themselves so Oprah would appear in the background of their shots.

And then someone was introducing me to Oprah, explaining that I had spoken at the summit. I thought I was in a dream. Oprah asked me my name and I rattled it off quickly. I was sweating; I was dying. I couldn't grasp the fact that I was talking to Oprah face-to-face. The place was loud, thumping with music and voices, and she asked me to repeat my name three times until she got it. I managed to tell her I was from Congo. Then she got pulled in another direction.

In addition to receiving an award, she introduced another award recipient, Jaycee Dugard, the young woman who had been kidnapped as a child and spent eighteen years locked up in the backyard of a pedophile.

Still reeling, I sat down next to a young woman and told her I liked her dress. She turned out to be singer Ingrid Michaelson, and she was performing at the event. She dedicated her first song to me. Another surreal moment. I met young activists from around the world that night—a girl who had started an all-female internet café in Afghanistan; a girl who had launched a major anti-bullying campaign in America.

On Monday, I went back to school like normal. But it was a new normal. The school had posted a notice about the summit on Facebook. People had watched the live-stream video from the event. Now everyone knew my deepest, darkest secrets. People came up to me, bursting with comments and questions.

"You're so brave."

"What was it like to meet Angelina?"

"I'm so sorry for what you've been through."

I didn't know many of the kids who approached me. But suddenly, they knew me, or thought they did. It was odd that people knew something about me when I knew nothing about them.

After that, all kinds of things happened. Humanitarian groups reached out to me, asking me to get involved. My photo exhibit began traveling to colleges around New York, mainly through word of mouth. Student organizations would hear about it and talk to school officials about bringing the exhibit to campus. I heard from old friends and relatives in Africa on Facebook. And I got messages from strangers around the world. I felt honored, and overwhelmed.

I heard from people in Kenya, Uganda, and Mozambique. People in a camp in Mozambique said they were Congolese Banyamulenge, just like me. "Can you help us?" they asked. I wanted to help them escape the camps. I realized they thought I was an influential figure in America, which of course I was not. I was a high school student. I'm sure people thought I lived a glamorous life in the States, hobnobbing with celebrities in the land where only good things happen. If only they knew.

TWENTY-FIVE

FIVE YEARS AFTER MY FAMILY MOVED TO
America, we had a major milestone: We were allowed to apply
for United States citizenship. We had never been considered
citizens of any country. We had always been stateless—not
citizens of Congo, not citizens of Rwanda. To get citizenship,
my parents and siblings had to study a list of facts about
American history, presidents, and politics, and then take a
test. I was seventeen years old at the time, which meant I
didn't have to take the test because I was under the age of
eighteen—I would become a citizen when my parents did.

I watched everyone do their homework for the test, using
the materials provided by officials. Every day my parents

listened to audio recordings of questions and answers: How many senators are in Congress? What are the three branches of government? They would play the questions over and over—at home, in the car, everywhere. It was kind of amusing, and also heartening, hearing my parents recite the branches of government in their broken English. They studied so hard.

Everyone passed the test. And for the first time in my life, I became a citizen of a country. I got a New York state ID. It was the first thing I owned that proved I exist.

It also meant that my family could vote—for the first time ever, anywhere. The concept of voting was foreign to us. Since we were not considered citizens in Congo, we could not vote. And even if we could, the system was so corrupt, it would have been futile. I couldn't believe that I would actually have a say in who makes the laws in America. My political views were beginning to take shape, and the more I learned about America, the more liberal I became. Sometimes I talked to my parents about my views, and theirs. Back home in Africa, my parents would have considered themselves conservative. I talked to them about the difference between liberals and conservatives in America, especially when it comes to issues of immigration, women, and human rights. They listened and learned with me. I became interested in laws that help immigrants in this country. This country was built on immigrants, after all. I also became interested in laws that protect human rights.

My senior year of high school, seventeen-year-old Trayvon Martin was shot dead in Florida. I watched the news unfold on TV with my mom: Trayvon, a black high school student, was walking home from a convenience store when a man named George Zimmerman began following him, deeming him suspicious. A scuffle ensued, and Zimmerman shot and killed him, claiming self-defense. Trayvon was unarmed. Mom and I both cried as we heard the story. The coverage immediately turned political, but at the heart of the story was this boy's grief-stricken parents. I kept thinking about his mom and dad, and how their lives would never be the same after losing their young son in such a violent way.

At school, the black girls were on top of the news, and we discussed it every day at lunch in the cafeteria. They followed every detail of the trial. Zimmerman was found not guilty.

It was another lesson on what it meant to be black in America. It's a harsh lesson to learn as a teen.

At the same time, it reminded me that there had never been any trial on behalf of my sister Deborah, or on behalf of any of my people who were killed. Our families had no chance to even try to get justice.

When I turned eighteen, I voted for Barack Obama. I was excited to be a part of politics in America, to have a voice. That year, I also won a Princeton Prize in Race Relations due to my photo exhibit and leadership at school. One of my teachers at Mercy, Miss Clasquin, had recommended me. She was a strong, fiery woman, and she always pushed me hard. I went to the awards conference at Princeton University and met kids from all over the country—American Muslims, Native Americans, African Americans. They shared their experiences, and I learned that there was so much discrimination toward all kinds of minorities in America. I hadn't realized how deeply rooted and wide-ranging it was. One black girl, a high school cheerleader, told me that the white captain of the squad was always talking down to her, as if she were a homeless person, when her parents were both doctors. Another black woman said she went to pick up a prescription at the pharmacy one day, and the clerk asked if she was on food stamps. I could see that I was just beginning to scratch the surface of understanding race in America.

I could also see that American kids had a hard time understanding that I was American. Kids at school would ask, "What are you?"

What am I? "I'm an American," I would say.

They would look at me skeptically. "Come on, what are you?"

When you hear questions like that, it makes you feel like you don't belong, like you have no right to claim American citizenship. I think it's why refugee kids often develop low expectations for their lives. Even as citizens, they feel like outsiders.

"Are you asking where I was born?" I would say. "If so, I was born in the Democratic Republic of the Congo. But now, I am an American."

What I often wanted to say was, "I'm a human being. What are you?"

TWENTY-SIX

THE SUMMER I GRADUATED FROM HIGH school, my sister Princesse planned to marry. She had met a lovely man from our tribe, and she decided to hold the wedding in Rwanda. I was excited to see Africa again, and to see my grandparents for the first time since I was a baby. I had been so young when I last saw them, in the mountains of South Kivu where my parents grew up, that I could not remember them. As my family planned the trip back to our homeland, I began to think about visiting a refugee camp. So many of my people were stuck in camps in Rwanda, displaced and stateless, living out their lives in tents. Some had reached out to me on Facebook, gaining access to computers wherever they could, like at internet cafés in nearby towns. I imagine that it took them forever to walk to those towns. And then they would have to find a way to pay for the internet access. I wanted to connect.

I floated the idea to Mom one afternoon while we were making tea in our kitchen. I tried to keep the conversation light, as I do when I say something Mom won't like. She looked bewildered.

"Why would you want to go back to a refugee camp?" she asked. "What if you have a mental breakdown?"

It was a fair question. I might have a meltdown. Mom probably didn't think I was serious.

"I would never go back to a camp," she said. I could understand that. She had been shot during the massacre, left for dead. She managed to walk away, but her youngest child did not.

She continued to cook, and I stopped talking about it. Mom didn't want to remember that hell. Me, I felt differently. Memories of Deborah and the massacre haunted me, lurking in the back of my mind. I wanted to conquer that fear. I wanted to visit a camp like the one where my family was attacked, to face down my past and see my people, forgotten by the world. Here in America, I had hope. I had a scholarship for college in the fall, where I would live on a beautiful campus, studying subjects I love. In America, I had books, and a bed to sleep on. I had a future. The night the man held a gun to my head, I thought I had no future. On that night, I said good-bye to my life. It's important to remember.

And also, it didn't feel right to stay away from a refugee camp because someone had attacked my family. People living in these isolated places need to know the outside world cares.

I decided that the only way my attackers could claim victory over me was if I let fear rule my life. So I made up my mind: I would go back to a camp. Princesse and Adele said they would go with me. They felt the same as I did. We picked a UN refugee camp near Kigali, the capital of Rwanda, where many of my people have been displaced due to conflict in Congo. My sisters and I wanted to go by ourselves, not in any official capacity with an organization, just us—arriving as friends, not foreigners. We planned to quietly visit the camp and talk with people about their lives. But my mother's concerns were valid: I didn't know if I would be able to cope. There was a chance I would panic when I saw the camp and need to turn right around. I had no idea how I would feel in that moment, but I knew one thing: I needed to find out.

When we landed in Kigali, I could see immediately that things had changed. Paved roads and highways stretched before us. There was a glossy new airport, towering skyscrapers. The city had evolved since I had last seen it, during those impoverished years when we lived in Rwanda after the massacre. Back then, more than five years earlier, the capital city was mired in corruption, with crumbling roads and buildings, slums in the middle of the city. Now on the city streets, the kids looked like American kids, busy with their cell phones, scrolling through Twitter and Facebook. Yet a few hours outside their city, children are living in a different universe, a refugee camp where water is the prized possession.

Before my sisters and I went to the camp, Mom warned us to be careful. "Don't spend the night," she said. She didn't understand why we were going, but she didn't try to stop us.

To get to the camp, my sisters and I took an early morning bus across the countryside, passing vast green valleys and hills, miles of tea fields, roadside vendors with baskets of fruit, boxy rural homes made of clay and cement. I remembered my own yellow home back when I was a girl in Uvira, where I played in the yard with my pet monkey. I loved seeing Africa again, speaking Swahili, not having to think about whether I was using the right words in English. There is something incredibly relaxing about Africa to me. Americans are always moving, always going somewhere, even if they have nothing important to do when they get there.

In Africa, you're generally home with your family, telling stories, making fun of one another, laughing.

The bus ride was long, and it reminded me of how isolated the refugee camps are. They are completely removed from society.

Some three bumpy hours later, we got off at a dusty corner. Men on motorbikes were hanging around by the side of the road, waiting to give people rides up a mountainside to the refugee camp. We agreed to pay a trio of young men to take us to the camp, and they handed us helmets. My sisters and I got on the backs of the bikes and sped away, holding on to our drivers.

It was the last week of July, dry and dusty, and I could feel the sun burning my skin. My jeans were soon covered in dust; my purple boots, brown. I covered my mouth with a scarf to protect myself from the dust. The road was so rugged, my helmet flew off when we went over a bump, and I had to hop off to retrieve it. Vendors dotted the roadside, staring as we passed. We had to stop and walk a few times, traversing rickety wooden bridges stretching across ponds. Women washed clothes in the ponds; children collected the water. My mind flew back to a memory of myself fetching water as a girl in the camp, but I didn't have time to think about it—we were heading toward an ominous rocky mountain that looked as if it went up into the clouds. As we hit the mountainside and drove higher and higher, my driver had to get off the bike sometimes and push it over the terrain. When I got back on the bike with him, I worried that we could roll backward, tumbling down the hill. I held on tight.

We made it to the camp, which was filled with tents as far as I could see. People walked toward us, eyeing us curiously. And I felt something different from what I had expected. Seeing the faces of my people, I experienced a rush of sudden joy. They all looked just like me. Even though they had never met me, they seemed to know me—they were my people. I didn't need to explain anything about myself like I do in America—my accent, my homeland, my heritage. They spoke my language, Kinyamulenge. They welcomed me because I was one of them. I was home.

At the same time, they seemed to know right away that we were from another world. Children ran up to us, staring and trailing us like we were celebrities. I had expected to blend in. But there was something that set us apart. On the faces of the people around us, I could see a universal expression, among the young and old—a look of hopelessness, a sense of resignation. This camp was their universe, and they had accepted that. My sisters and I had arrived with hope in our eyes. We looked different.

The sounds and memories of my own childhood refugee camp came rushing back—children playing, pots banging. Women cooked on clay stoves outside; babies cried. Camp officials, we learned from a group of teenage boys, were in the midst of a "drug cleansing" that day. Outsiders had brought drugs to the camp to sell them to young men. How awful, I thought, for drug dealers to try to get poor people hooked on drugs. The officials walked around the camp, burning the drugs in front of people. There were kids playing dodgeball with makeshift balls made of wadded-up plastic shopping bags, tied together with shoelaces—the same kinds of balls we played with as kids. I hadn't thought about those balls in years.

Outside a tent, a young girl in a pink T-shirt and long skirt dutifully swept the entrance with a broom.

"Hello," I said, walking up to her. "I'm Sandra. What is your name?"

"Francine," she said.

"And how old are you?"

"Thirteen."

She had short hair like I did as a girl, and it sent me soaring back to my childhood again. I saw myself in Francine; I was a little younger than her when I was in the camp, and she carried herself as I did. She didn't talk much, unlike the other kids who brazenly followed us around the camp. She told me it was her job to do chores for the family, like caring for her little brother and fetching water each morning from the public fountain. She said she had lived in the camp for seven years, more than half her life. She told me she went to school, walking an hour up and down the hill each way to get there, and I was glad to hear it.

"What do you want to do when you finish school?" I asked her.

"I don't know," she said, as if she had never even thought about it.

I pressed her. "Surely you must dream of something?"

She couldn't think of one single thing she wanted. She had no dreams. I encouraged her to think about what interested her, and what she might want to do when she grows up.

Finally, after some thought, she said maybe she could be a nurse in the camp one day, caring for children. She couldn't visualize a life outside the camp.

I told her, "You know, you could be a nurse in a hospital, in the city, or somewhere beyond the camp."

She couldn't imagine it. That was a world she did not know.

"Your life doesn't have to be here," I said. "It doesn't have to end here." My eyes welled up at the thought of it. She noticed and watched me curiously. She must have thought I was crazy.

We walked together for a few minutes, and then she had to return home to her chores. I took pictures of the two of us, thanked her for talking with me, and said good-bye. It broke my heart a little to see her walk away.

Across the way, a woman who looked a little younger than my mother welcomed us into her tent. Inside, there was no furniture, just mats on the ground for sleeping. Curtains served as walls between rooms. She said she had lived there for several years, along with her children. She asked if I wanted any water or food, and the offer could not have been more generous. There, water is the best gift you can give—a precious commodity. It is the difference between life and death, not something you drink at your leisure. To get water, people have to walk about thirty minutes down a hill to the fountain, stand in line, fill a bucket, and walk back. I accepted the water because it would have been rude to say no. Then I let my mind take me back to my own treks for water as a girl in the refugee camp in Gatumba—the long lines, the fights, the bullies pushing me to the end of the line. I remembered how I longed to return to school. Back then, I never imagined how my life would change.

As we continued to walk around the camp, a man kept staring at us. He seemed to recognize us, but I had never seen him before. He stopped us and spoke to Princesse.

"Murabana ba Raheri," he said. "Are you Rachel's children?"

"Yego," Princesse replied. "Yes."

"Yooooo!" he exclaimed. I tried to recall his face.

"Ndi nyokorome," he said. "I'm your uncle!"

"Nibyo?" Princesse asked. "Is that so?"

In our culture, if someone says you're related, even if you don't know the person, you respond with respect. We smiled and listened to him. I don't think anyone recognized him, not even Adele, who usually knows everyone. He told us that his father and my grandpa are brothers. He said he had been close to my mother in Congo. He didn't know how many of us had survived the attack. He had heard that my mom had lost some of her children. He hugged us tightly, then took us inside his home and offered us some food.

And, again, I was transported back to Gatumba, reliving the tasteless food, the confined spaces. Our uncle told us stories of our mother and introduced us to his family. I wanted so badly to remove them from the camp. I could imagine all the fear, isolation, and hopelessness they must be feeling. No one deserves to watch life pass them by in a camp.

The day moved too quickly into evening, and it was time to go.

"Say hello to your mom," my uncle told us. "Tell her you saw your uncle. She will know exactly who you are talking about."

My sisters and I said farewell to all of our new friends, a sentimental moment, as we were leaving them behind. We roared back down the mountainside on motorbikes, and a bus eventually rolled up, crowded with dozens of people. We squished ourselves into the seats, exhausted from the day. I thought about how when you grow up in a refugee camp, you don't know how terrible the camp is because you have never known anything better. I thought about Francine, the girl with no dreams. She wasn't growing up expecting things like basic human rights, a real home, or a future.

As night fell over the hushed, shadowy hills of the countryside, I thought of the women in the camp, spending their days cooking with corn and rice, tending to their children, gossiping about camp life. I thought of their husbands, desperately seeking day labor in the city, trying to find any work that they could. I thought about how my family had been resettled because of the massacre. Officials were worried about retaliation after the attack, and so we were given an opportunity to leave the country and start anew. If it hadn't been for the massacre, I could still be living in a camp like that. But also, if it hadn't been for the massacre, I would still have my sister Deborah.

My sisters and I sat silently on the bus as warm, dusty air blew in through the windows. We had wanted to record a cell phone video to document our feelings about our experience that day. But there were no words.

TWENTY-SEVEN

THE NIGHT BEFORE MY SISTER'S WEDDING IN Rwanda, we attended a big party to celebrate the giving away of the bride. Our elders told stories, kids danced, and women cooked an entire cow—at the party, you're supposed to eat a whole cow. I saw relatives I had not seen since I was a child, and I met some new ones I had never seen before. Because my family now lived in America, everyone assumed we were rich, which I thought was funny. A few people asked us for bus fare.

I relished seeing the familiar faces of my relatives, and I essentially met my grandparents for the first time. I could not remember meeting them in the mountains when I was a baby.

I met my grandpa on my dad's side and my grandma on my mom's side. The others had passed away. It was fascinating to spend time with my grandparents and see where my parents got their personalities.

My grandmother looked very much like my mom, and I could also see where Mom got her strength. Grandma had raised four daughters and four sons, and she was a true matriarch: Her husband had died after my mom got married, and she cared for the family on her own. Mom had once told me that when Grandma was raising her kids, she hadn't really seen the logic in educating girls. She thought they would just get married and take their knowledge to another family. That was the way her generation thought—simply part of the culture. But years later, after Mom started her own business and put all her girls through school, encouraging us to learn and grow, Grandma said that she could see the value in girls. It was a big moment for Mom.

Grandma was funny and sarcastic like Mom too. The first thing she said when she met me: "Oh, you turned out short." And then, "I wasn't sure that you were going to grow up to be pretty."

I said, "Grandma, you just met me!"

My grandfather was just like my dad—sweet and serene. He told me that he had been following my activism. A radio show in Congo had discussed my appearance at the Women in the World Summit, and he had heard it in his village. Such a small world! "We hear about all the good things you're doing for our community," he said. However, he joked that I had also caused some problems for him: The people in his village thought he must be rich since his granddaughter was hobnobbing with American celebrities.

"Since you're so wealthy, I brought a bag for you to fill with money," he said with a laugh. "I'll bring it back to the village."

I was pleasantly surprised by his support of my activism. Like my grandmother, he had once believed that girls did not need to be educated. He had worried that my mom was too educated for my dad when they wed, and of course, she had attended school for just a few years. But clearly he had evolved, just like my grandma.

Princesse's wedding was immense, with hundreds of people arriving. Everyone always brings their entire family, all their cousins and aunties and uncles, to the ceremony, no matter how many people you invite. I wore a peachy silk bridesmaid dress and beaded necklace. I had such a phenomenal time, I did not want to go home.

But I had to get ready for college.

That fall, I packed my bags and left for Houghton College,

a Christian university not far from home in New York. My sister Princesse had gone there, so we knew the school well. My parents liked the idea that I would be close to home. They would have preferred that I live at home and commute to school, but I wanted to live on campus. It was time for me to go.

At first, I loved it. Away from home for the first time, I felt independent. I had a roommate named Meredith, a quiet, sweet person, the perfect roommate—almost too perfect! I quickly met an African girl wearing awesome braids. Petite and cute, she said her name was Mary Louise. She had been adopted by a missionary couple on the Ivory Coast. I started calling her "Nugget," a nickname my sisters had once given me. Before long, everyone called her Nugget.

She introduced me to a girl in my dorm named Shannon, and we became friends right away. Shannon had grown up in a conservative Christian family in a small town near Rochester. She had recently reconnected with her dad after a difficult divorce. Tall, a bit shy and clumsy, she was incredibly warm and friendly, with kind eyes and a big smile.

I met another good friend in a digital-imaging class. The professor had told us to find a subject and go take some portraits. I looked at this gorgeous girl named Kaya, who had midnight-black hair, pale skin, blue eyes. We left the class together to find subjects for our portraits, and nabbed some boys in the hall who were game. An artist from California, she seemed free-spirited and fun. We soon became inseparable.

A guy named Philip rounded out my eclectic group of friends. He was the openly gay son of a pastor from Pennsylvania, and I met him through a mutual friend one day when we needed a ride off campus. Philip had a car and offered to drive us, and I sat with him up front. He asked me to feed him jelly beans as we drove, and a friendship was born.

I made friends easily, in part because Princesse had gone to the school, but also because people recognized me from choir performances we had held there over the years. The campus newspaper had also run a piece about my appearance at the Women in the World Summit. So some people knew about my history before I met them. Strangers would come up to me and say, "Hi, Sandra," as if they knew me already. Other times, random people would approach and give me a hug. I knew nothing about them, but they knew something about me. I wasn't sure if I wanted my past to be the first thing people knew about me. I realized I couldn't introduce myself like a regular person and let people get to know me. But I also knew that this was a result of my activism, and it was a new reality I needed to accept.

It happened to my mom too. One day she came to visit the campus and was in a public bathroom when a student approached her and said, "Are you Sandra's mom?" Mom nodded, and the girl gave her a big hug and started to cry. Mom was totally mystified. She didn't know much English, and she had no idea what was going on. Later she said, "Sandra, what did you do? Why did this girl hug me and start crying?" I had to explain that the girl must have heard about our past, presumably from my appearance at the summit.

My activism had caught the attention of some men in my culture too. Some of the older men were concerned that a young woman was speaking for our tribe. I didn't see it that way—I was just telling my story in the hopes that it would help people understand my experience. But the men weren't sure what to think. They would call my dad and ask about what I planned to say in my next speech. I had begun talking to refugee groups, and I posted details about the events on Facebook. The men did not think I was qualified. They saw me as a child. Dad relayed the messages to me, but told me not to worry. "Do what you want. Say what you want," he said.

No one in my family ever tried to direct what I said. Sometimes they would give me advice—for instance, Mom once suggested that I explain that there was no one to protect us from the attackers in the refugee camp—but they let me find my own voice. The younger generation of my tribe, meanwhile, totally cheered me on.

On campus, I developed a brief romance with a guy who was a tattoo artist named Xavier. He was a lost soul, and we connected because I was a bit lost too at the time. Xavier gave me a tiny tattoo of a black heart on my collarbone, and I loved it. I had always wanted a tattoo, and I was finally free to get one. I picked a black heart because it reflected my innermost thoughts—that everything I held dear was tainted and dark. I managed to hide the tattoo from my parents when I saw them on the weekends—until one Sunday at church. I wore a blouse that revealed the heart. A woman at church noticed it and said, "That's so cute!" She turned to my mother, telling her how adorable it was. Thanks a lot! I don't know why she needed to point it out to my mom.

Mom looked at it and said, "No." She reached out and tried to rub it off.

"Mom, let's not get angry," I said. "The tattoo is there. It's not going away."

She sighed heavily. My poor mom. I dragged her through hell with my American ways.

Eventually, life on campus got complicated. The majority of students were white, and again there was a racial divide.

I first encountered it with a girl named Angel in my dormitory. She was white, like most girls in the dorm. I didn't know her, except to say hello when we crossed paths on campus. One day she was crying in the hallway. I asked her if she was okay, and she looked at me strangely. She actually said these words: "Can I touch you?" She said she had never touched a black person. I humored her, and let her touch me. She closed her eyes and announced, while stroking my arm, "Wow, if I close my eyes, it's like you're white."

She was astonished that my skin felt like hers. I laughed and said, "Do not ever try that with any other black kids. They will not be so amused. They will knock you flat!"

Then she wanted to touch my hair, which was in braids. Again, I said, "Do not try any of these things with other black kids!" She had come from a tiny rural town with no black people. It would be the first of many such incidents for me on campus.

I had been looking forward to college because I thought I would be meeting a diverse range of people. I was excited to be independent and to experience life without my parents' watchful eyes. I wanted to make new friends, to feel like an average American teen. I was finally out of high school, so the "no boys until you graduate" rule from my parents had been lifted. And my brother Alex was not around to shoo away every boy who coughed in my direction. But I quickly realized that there was a definite type at Houghton: white skin, long beautiful hair, everything that I didn't have. For the most part, white boys liked white girls, and black boys liked white girls. There was no space for my dark skin. I had male friends of both races, but I felt more like an accessory to enhance their coolness factor than a pretty girl they could ask out on a date.

One day I called my mother, sobbing. She asked me what was wrong, and I had no answer for her. I didn't know what was wrong. I thought that if I told her that I didn't feel beautiful, she would find it silly and dismiss it. Instead of sharing my feelings, I cried and told her I missed home.

One night at a college dance, I was talking with a cute boy. But then a flirty girl swooped in and pulled him away. I knew her, and I had thought she was a friend, although I could see that she was self-absorbed. Her name was Donna, and she thought she was hot—she thought she was all that and a bag of chips. She whisked the guy off and started dancing with him, and that was the end of that short-lived romance for me. It was also the end of my friendship with her.

Later, I met a white guy who seemed interested in me—until he said: "Sandra, you're so pretty for a black girl." What? There's a difference between pretty black girls and pretty white girls? I wish I had said: "Wow, you're pretty stupid for a college student."

He hurt me with his remark. He didn't see me, just my skin color. But my friends were there for me. When they heard what he said, they stopped talking to him.

I had heard similar comments about my looks before. I was learning about shades of black in America, and about how your skin tone determines where you stand on the beauty scale. Americans are so nutty about physical appearance and what defines beauty. Basically, the lighter skinned you are, and the smaller and straighter your nose is, the "prettier" you are.

I also began to understand why hair is such an important issue for African American women. I learned why the black girls in school didn't let their hair grow naturally, but instead always straightened or relaxed it. My black friends explained that since they were already considered second tier to white women in the looks department, it was important not to have unruly hair. Black hair, in its natural state, is "nappy" and disorderly, they told me. They said, "You can't have your natural hair out." They said black women have to keep their hair tidy and straight, like white women, if they want to be taken seriously at work and in school. Again, I said, "What? This is crazy."

These were issues I never had to deal with in Africa. There, my sisters and I wore our hair short and never gave it a second thought. We didn't have to worry about natural hair versus straightened hair; we didn't worry about our hair at all. But in America, it was a very big issue. And so, in order to fit in, as all teens want to do, I usually wore my hair in braids or straightened it with chemicals, sometimes burning my scalp if I left the chemicals on for too long.

I didn't understand how the hair that grew out of my head could be considered messy. I occasionally wore my hair out in its natural state, big and puffy. I've come to love my hair, but at the time, when I wore it as an Afro, it sparked a lot of unwanted conversation. People thought I was making a statement, when I was simply wearing my natural hair. They would examine it and say things like:

"Do you tease your hair?"

"Ooh, your hair is so cool—can I touch it?"

"Oh wow, how do you get your hair to do that?"

White girls would sink their hands in my Afro and smile as if they were petting me. Not only did they make me feel like an exotic animal, but they also messed up my hair. How would they feel if I ran my fingers through their hair?

It was easiest to wear braids. I didn't have the time or money to spend hours straightening my hair before class.

Braids are easy to maintain, but they do hurt like mad for a few days until they settle. The first night after you have them done, you have to find a creative way to sleep, such as on your forehead. Of course, people thought I was making a statement by wearing braids too. They thought everything about my appearance was a statement, when I was simply wearing clothes, going to class, doing my daily routine. I really stuck out at Houghton. If I wore one of my African skirts or dresses, people would look me up and down and say things like:

"Oh wow, what's the occasion?"

"You look like an African goddess."

I wanted to say, "Come on now, it's just a skirt. It's not revolutionary." I know that people meant well. I tried to laugh it off. Sometimes I just said, "Yeah, I'm an African goddess."

To help us all understand one another, I became president of the Black History Club on campus. We decided to do a photo exhibit with some of the black students to help people get to know us a little better. We took portraits and did brief write-ups for everyone—little introductions with a few details about our lives and interests. We called the exhibit "Shades of Black." When the exhibit opened, an idiot student decided it would be hilarious to change the sign to "50 Shades of Light Black" and drape paper chains all over the walls—a nod to the book *Fifty Shades of Grey*. But when the black students came in and saw the chains, as you can imagine, they felt incredibly insulted. We were trying to honor black students, and someone had filled the room with symbols of slavery. The kids started crying.

I went to the dean. He knew me by now. I had spoken with him before about inappropriate comments on campus and ways to make minorities feel more at home. When I arrived at his office, I could see from the look on his face that he was thinking, Uh-oh, what now? I told him about the chains strung across the portraits. I explained that this was devastating for the black students on campus. I said, "What are we going to do about this?" To add to the urgency, I said we needed to do something before everyone started tweeting about it. School officials promptly looked at the campus security cameras and figured out who did it, although they didn't release the student's name immediately. It was a white boy. He had to apologize and he got suspended, but that didn't feel like enough. This student did something that he thought his peers were going to find funny. This was a small manifestation of a much larger issue on campus. These kinds of antics were not what I expected from my college experience.

After that, I called my mom and burst into tears.

"What's wrong?" she asked. "Do you want to come home?"

"Mom, I don't want to be here," I said. "I don't think they like black people."

"We can come get you," she said. I'm sure she was confused: She knew I never had any problems making friends.

Suddenly I didn't feel like getting into all the details with her. I didn't want to worry her, and I didn't want her to think I couldn't handle college. I calmed down and said I would be fine.

I really wanted to leave the school, but I stayed. Someone had to push for change.

I got more involved. I joined a committee with the dean and others to establish a diversity program. We held a range of cultural events, like a soul-food night, a movie night with films about civil-rights movements, a Caribbean night, a Motown dance. Our goal was to show people diversity within the black community. We also held weekly meetings to talk about current issues, and everyone was welcome to come and ask questions.

It helped me survive my freshman year. But a much bigger battle was yet to come.

TWENTY-EIGHT

WHEN I WENT BACK TO SCHOOL FOR MY sophomore year, I did so with dread. I was exhausted by the thought of dealing with more racial chasms. I tried to remind myself that getting my education was the top priority and that I should stay focused. My parents had always stressed the importance of my studies. I agreed that getting my college degree was paramount, but I wanted to do it in an environment where I could feel comfortable.

This was the year my past caught up with me.

I had experienced nightmares in the past, but they began to grow stronger—shattering images flooding back from the massacre. I would wake up screaming. In one dream, I visited the remains of the refugee camp at Gatumba with Mom, and I sobbed at seeing the bloody scene. I walked alongside a row of caskets, trying to feel my sister Deborah's energy. But I couldn't, so Mom showed me a casket with her remains. I leaned over it and cried. I hugged the casket and refused to leave. When I woke up, my whole body was aching. It felt as if I had been crying all night. Of course, Deborah never even had a casket: Her remains were scooped up and thrown in a plastic bag. Who knows where that bag wound up; probably in a ditch somewhere with a pile of other bags of bones.

Another night, a dream took me right back to the night we were attacked. I was there in the camp, surrounded by men with torches and machetes. I woke up screaming. My friend Shannon, who was now my roommate, heard me. She and Kaya stayed up with me all night long, trying to make me feel safe. They were my two closest friends, so loyal and loving.

Pretty soon the nightmares hit during the day—flashbacks. I would be sitting in class and a bloody image from the massacre would come, assaulting my mind. I would enter another zone, wrapped in despair. My friend Philip saw it happen to me and said I looked like a zombie. I lost sleep. I tried to stay up all night, afraid to let the nightmares get me in bed. But they got to me anyway, at all times of the day and night. I was worn out. My personality changed. I became depressed, lethargic. My friends asked where my bubbly personality had gone. My grades started slipping. I had always been a good student, but I began doing terribly in school. I couldn't concentrate on anything. I became paralyzed by worries of when the flashbacks would come. They took over my life.

I didn't tell my parents. They had always been so strong. They had been through a lifetime of tragedy and war, and they always managed to keep going. I was afraid they would be disappointed. They had worked hard to give me opportunities in life. I couldn't let them down. I thought I should be strong like them. I should be embracing my chance to get a college degree, not melting down about my past. I didn't think my parents would understand.

I just didn't know how to tell them what was happening. We didn't even have the language to talk about mental illness in my culture. The idea of talking to a therapist about our feelings was foreign. Some of my friends in high school had talked to therapists, and I had always thought that was odd. I didn't understand the concept of paying a stranger to listen to you. It's not something we did. And my family had never talked about the massacre, even among ourselves. So I kept it all to myself.

But I couldn't keep it from my closest friends. They saw me sinking. Shannon would go to class and return to find me lying in bed. She would ask if I had gone to class myself, and I would say, "No. Just turn off the lights." I stopped going out with my friends, and they started taking turns staying in with me at night, babysitting me. One day I told Shannon I didn't know why I was alive, and she got so worried about me, she reported me to the residency director. I was mad at her for doing that, but I know she did it because she cared. She did not know what else to do. She told me she was afraid I was going to commit suicide. I didn't want to kill myself, but I didn't really want to exist either. It felt like that the first month after the massacre, like it was too exhausting to exist. I was sleepless but tired, all the time. If someone came up behind me suddenly or startled me, I jumped out of my skin. The residency director began checking on me three times a day, and said I needed to see a counselor.

Here's the thing about flashbacks: They don't give warnings. They just show up, unannounced, unprovoked. You could be having a great day, and then, out of nowhere, dreadful images start filling your head. The next thing you know, you're on the floor, curled up in the fetal position, unable to remember how you got there. Your limbs ache and your ears ring, as if you were right back in that awful place you tried so hard to forget. Your body shivers, even when you're indoors and the temperature is seventy-five degrees. You don't want to call anyone who might understand, like your mom or your siblings, because you don't want to ruin their day. So you end up crying to your friends. But you can't find the words to explain that you can never visit your sister's grave, because she has no grave. It feels like you want to scream, but your lungs fail. How do you explain to someone that you're grieving now because you never had the chance to do so as a child?

I started seeing a campus counselor, because the residency director had said it was necessary. I was reluctant to talk to him at first. What could he possibly know about what I had been through? I showed up for the first session, determined to tell him nothing. I decided I would sit there until the time was up.

"Hi, Sandra," he said. "How are you?"

"I'm fine," I said.

"Your friends don't think you are," he said.

I smiled, implying that my friends were being silly. "I'm fine," I said again.

"Just so you know, you don't need to be fine in this office," he said.

"Really, I'm fine."

He started asking questions—about my relationship with

my family, about why my friends were concerned about me. I kept smiling, trying to act casual, giving simple yes or no answers and saying I was fine.

"This is just between you and me," he said, attempting to get me to open up. "No one at the school needs to know that we are talking."

"I'm fine," I said.

I didn't look him in the face. I looked everywhere but there. I looked at a decorative fountain in his office—a mini waterfall trickling over rocks. I played with a little sandbox on the table next to me, drawing swirls in the sand with my fingers.

Pretty soon, the first session was up. But he was patient and persistent. At the next session, he said he knew about my activism, and he asked me about that. We talked about the Foundation of Hope Ministries, and he asked if I saw myself doing more humanitarian work in the future. At first I continued to give him brief answers, but then I started talking a little more, telling him about how I would like to help displaced people.

Gradually, he put me at ease by simply listening.

Worries and doubts began spilling forth that I didn't even know had been lodged deep inside of my mind. I talked about how I didn't understand why I had survived the massacre

240

when Deborah had not. I said that sometimes I feared that my parents blamed me for Deborah's death. I don't know where I got that idea, but it was there. I expressed how much I hated being called the youngest in my family because it implied that Deborah never existed. I hated the fact that my whole family was treating her like some distant figure from our past, when her energy, memories, and face were all I thought about. Every time Mom introduced me as her youngest, I died a little inside. I felt so guilty, like I was taking Deborah's place—something I would never dream of doing. My parents behaved like she was really dead, and I wasn't ready for that. I didn't want her to be dead to us; I wanted to keep her memory alive. I wanted everyone I met to know that there was a beautiful little girl whose life was stolen and that she is my little sister—she would always be my little sister.

After the sessions, I would feel so tired and drained, I would go back to my dorm room and sleep.

Amid all of this emotional chaos, I received an invitation to speak to the United Nations Security Council about children and armed conflict. The invitation came through a group called RefugePoint, which works on behalf of global refugees. The cofounder, Sasha Chanoff, has been a vocal advocate for the Banyamulenge. After the Gatumba massacre, he went to the State Department to propose that the survivors be resettled. I had met him at one of the annual reunions of my people.

Sasha asked if I would like to speak to the UN. It was an intimidating prospect—I would be talking to people who make decisions for the entire world. But I knew it was a powerful platform, and I wanted to tell my story. And so I did.

When I sat down before the council, Samantha Power, the United States Ambassador to the UN, introduced me to the audience. Trying to remain calm, I started by talking about my history. "My ancestors are from Rwanda. For many generations, my family lived in the Democratic Republic of the Congo, where I was born. Still, many Congolese considered my people to be Rwandan because of the language that we speak and the way that we look," I said.

"We were born into war," I continued, describing my childhood. "I got used to dropping out of school and fleeing every time a new war broke out." Then I recalled the terrors of the camp in Gatumba. "I was about ten years old. We had been there for a few months when it happened. I remember it vividly. It's nighttime. I am woken up with what sounds like popcorn popping. My mother is frantically telling me to wake up. I open my eyes and I see fear in her face. Then I see my aunt standing next to her, blood running down her arm like a stream and gushing onto my leg."

As I concluded, I said, "That is my story. I will tell it to anyone who will listen. Not because it is easy. Every time I tell it, I am back in Gatumba, a ten-year-old burning in a tent. But as long as the criminal who admitted to leading that massacre continues to walk freely in the streets of Burundi, I have no choice. I must keep telling it, until the international community proves my words are not only worthy of empathy, but also of accountability. Until leaders like you and the countries that you represent show me that my family and all others are not disposable."

I called on the council to bring the killers to justice. "Only then will millions of survivors like me hear loud and clear that our lives have value," I said. "Until there is justice, the nightmares will never stop."

And then I went back to school, back to the nightmares.

My friends tried to help me through it. They would leave funny little Post-it Notes around the room to cheer me up. Girls on my floor wrote me letters too, expressing their love and support. They could see the change in me. I kept spiraling, and I kept going to the counselor.

In late December, the time came to go home for Christmas break. But when I talked to Dad on the phone about it, I panicked. If I went home, my parents would see that I had become an emotional mess. They would wonder what was going on and ask a million questions. I was afraid to tell them about the flashbacks. I was flunking out of my classes. I did not want to return to school for the second semester, but I couldn't imagine telling my parents such a thing. Education meant the world to them. I feared they would not understand.

I told my counselor I did not want to go home. I asked him if he would send my parents a reassuring note, explaining that I would be staying with a friend for Christmas break. He did so. Later, I texted my dad, who was confused. I had never been away from home for Christmas.

"Hey, Dad, don't pick me up. I'm not coming home," I said. "I just need to go somewhere else. I just need to go get better."

"Get better from what?" Dad asked. "What are you talking about? You need to come home. We'll pray for you." To my dad, prayers can fix everything.

"You can pray, but I might need more than that," I said.

"Are you saying God is not capable?"

"No," I said. "That's not what I'm saying."

I paced around the room with my phone. I didn't feel comfortable telling my dad what was happening with me. I didn't want to hurt or worry my parents, but I needed to get away. Shannon was in the room with me, packing for her own trip home, giving me sympathetic looks. I told Dad I would be staying with a friend for the holidays. I wasn't explaining myself well, but I knew that I did not want to go home and try to explain everything to my parents. In my culture, people don't talk to each other about their innermost thoughts and feelings.

I went to stay with a friend who lived near campus for Christmas. Shannon had offered to let me stay with her, but I knew my parents would find me there.

Over the holidays, while staying at my friend's house, I called a friend I had met through a nonprofit group, the Women's Refugee Commission. Her name was Diana, and she lived in New York City. She generously said I could stay with her and her husband after Christmas, as their son would be away at school for the semester. I decided that's what I would do. I did not know how long I would stay, but I knew I would not be going back to college for that next semester.

My parents were in turmoil. Mom texted me a note: *Sandra, I know you're pregnant. Just come home.*

That was the final blow. I was heartbroken. I knew I hadn't explained my feelings to my parents, but did she need to jump to that conclusion? I shut off my phone.

I went to my friend's place for Christmas. My parents did not know where I was staying. They asked Shannon to tell them. A loyal friend, she didn't divulge anything. I didn't want to worry my parents, but I knew that if I went home, I would see everything from their perspective. I needed to find my own perspective.

Then my parents called the police. The officers asked Shannon where I was, and she still wouldn't tell them. Bless her heart, Shannon was such a good girl, she had never even had a drop of alcohol, and here she was, defying the police for me. I was over the age of eighteen, so the police couldn't make me go home. But they wanted to soothe my parents, and they asked Shannon if she would give them a phone number so they could call me. They assured her that they would not give the number to my parents.

She gave them the number, and the police called and asked me, "Are you safe?" I said yes. I explained that I did not want to be at home for personal reasons. I told them, "Please tell my parents I am safe. Tell them not to worry."

In January, I boarded a bus bound for New York City.

TWENTY-NINE

AFTER AROUND EIGHT HOURS ON THE BUS, we pulled into the Port Authority Bus Terminal in New York City, an enormous, labyrinthine building in the middle of the city. When I arrived, I had a brief sense of relief to be on my own, away from college, away from my parents. No one would try to lecture me about anything here. I found my way to the subway station and took a train out to Brooklyn, where my friend Diana lived. When I made it to her place, I crashed. I had no plan.

Diana lived in Park Slope, a trendy neighborhood of cafés and shops, but I could barely leave the apartment. I slept a lot, and cried. Soon, I was crying all the time. I had no routine. I wanted to find a job, but I was too depressed to do much of anything. It was a brutally cold winter, with temperatures slipping under zero degrees at night. I stayed inside, hunkered under a blanket. I didn't contact my parents, but I posted updates on my Facebook page so they would know I was safe, and I kept in touch sporadically with my siblings.

One day Princesse called and asked what I was doing with my life. She said she had spoken to a professor at Houghton—one of my favorite professors, a woman from Kenya—to ask her why I had left school. The professor told Princesse that she thought I had become distracted by superficial things, such as makeup and clothes. She thought I didn't have my priorities straight and that I couldn't keep up with my studies, so that's why I had left. I had always looked up to this woman, but here she was, making assumptions about me when she had no idea what I was experiencing. She didn't know about the flashbacks, the depression. She was the one being superficial: She thought I looked good on the outside, so everything must be fine on the inside. It was such a betrayal. I sank even lower.

Diana tried to help, recommending that I apply for a free treatment program at a trauma center in Manhattan. I did, but I was put on a long waiting list and never received a call. As much as I wanted to climb out of the fog, I couldn't find a way to do it. I had no money for therapy. I was still plagued by flashbacks, living in fear of when the next one would hit.

My best friends from college—Shannon, Kaya, and Philip—stayed in touch and tried to encourage me, but I was lost. I started writing poetry, and also prayers. In my prayers, I did not ask for things, but instead, thanked God for things. I thought it might help my state of mind. I thanked God that I was still alive. I thanked him for my friends. I thanked him for my parents and their love, even though I was mad at them. I thanked him that my parents were still alive.

I wrote down thoughts and memories, trying to find my way back. In one series of notes, I wrote: *I still don't fully under-stand death, but I envy everyone who at least got to bury their loved one. I envy everyone who gets to visit graves, bring flowers to them on birthdays and anniversaries. Deborah was buried in a mass grave with approximately 166 other people. I have never visited her grave. Come to think of it, I have never visited anyone's grave, not even my favorite uncle's grave. I don't know where he's buried, just like I don't really know where Deborah is buried. It's such a weird thing to envy, but every time I see people carry caskets, I think of how lucky they are, and I wish I could have been that lucky. No one can anticipate death, not even when people are very sick; when they take their last breath, it's still the punch in the gut that you can never be ready for. What you can get ready for is showing your loved one the respect and love that you think they deserve. If Deborah had a grave, I'd make sure that the flowers on it never died. My baby sister was disposed of, not buried. She was slaughtered like an animal and buried like one.*

My writing helped me sort through my feelings, but I had a long way to go to feel hopeful again. My friend Kaya came to visit and started crying when she saw how dejected I looked. I could see that she felt helpless, and this made me feel bad too. The two of us just sat and cried. Finally, she said, "We need to do something to make you feel better."

First she made me go on the dating app Tinder. She thought it might help if I met some new people. Then she took me out dancing at a lively Hispanic restaurant and club. There, we listened to music—Prince Royce, Enrique Iglesias— and danced. I managed to make myself smile, even if I didn't feel entirely happy.

Soon after, I started chatting with a guy on Tinder. A handsome Italian guy named Rocco, he was a charmer with dark brown hair and light brown eyes. At the time, he had just dropped out of college and was living on nearby Long Island, working as an electrician. He was trying to find something he felt passionate about in life. He reminded me a lot of myself— we were both unsure what to do with ourselves.

Our first date was in February, the day after Valentine's Day. He had wanted to take me out on Valentine's Day, but I said, "No, that's weird. That's what couples do! We are just getting to know each other."

He took me to a fancy Italian restaurant in Brooklyn, and he looked nervous, fidgeting with his hands. His nervousness made me relax. He seemed like a nice guy. As he became more comfortable, we began to laugh about random things. We noticed that people in the restaurant kept looking at my hair. It was in braids, and I had woven the braids into one big braid. Finally, a guy at the next table said, "Oh my God, girl, you are fabulous!" Rocco and I laughed. We had the same sense of humor, and we were ready for things to be easy. We clicked.

Our romance bloomed quickly. We talked often. We helped each other escape the reality of our uncertain lives, but also, we helped each other think about some important issues. We talked about our challenges and how we were trying to find our place in the world. It helped me to have someone listen, with my college friends far away. He was gentle, and I could be honest and forthright with him, and he would not judge me. I opened up to him about my past and about my struggles with flashbacks. I had always worried that guys would shy away when they heard about my history. But he did the opposite. He encouraged me to talk about my feelings and experiences. He was such a refreshing surprise in my life.

Within two weeks of our first date, I met his family and his puppy, Oliver. His family was kind to me, and accepting. They welcomed me and made me feel right at home. I learned that people in his family hadn't really dated outside of their culture, but they embraced me anyway. I thought about how my family would probably not be so accepting of him. They wanted me to marry within my culture. They would not approve of my dating a white Italian guy. They would not approve of my dating at all.

I was envious that Rocco had grown up in America, a place where people could date across cultures and it was not an issue. He and I had some uncomfortable conversations about my family and about how they might not accept him in the way that his family had accepted me. It was difficult for me to explain, and I could see that it pained him to hear it. But he tried to understand. He didn't let it come between us. He was bighearted. If I were in his situation, hearing about a family that might not want me around, I would have thought, I don't know if I want to date this person. But he accepted me.

I spent weekends with his family. His mom and I would sit in the living room and watch cheesy romantic movies, like *Safe Haven* starring Julianne Hough. We drank wine and laughed at the corny lines. Rocco's home and his family started to feel familiar, kind of like my own family. He and I walked on the beach and talked deep into the evenings, and I cried as I told him how lost I felt. There were nights where we'd be sleeping and I would start to cry and he would just hold me and tell me he was there and that everything was going to be all right. He never distanced himself or treated me any differently, no matter what I said. He didn't tiptoe around my feelings. He addressed them head-on. He supported me. And he remained playful and sweet. I think you meet people you need at crucial times in your life, and he was one of those people. His presence in my life meant so much to me. At a time when I needed a family but could not deal with my own, he gave me the family I craved.

I began to come back to myself. You can't help but feel happy when people show you love and support. His parents played a tremendous role in my recovery, and they probably didn't even know it. They were just being themselves, a caring family. Their love, along with my independence from college and home, helped me clear my mind. I had needed time and distance to think about things for myself. Little by little, the flashbacks began to recede. One day, I realized that a couple weeks had passed without a flashback.

Rocco encouraged me to fix things with my family. We talked about that a lot. He kept saying he would drive me to Rochester to see my mom and dad.

Meanwhile, my parents had seen pictures of him on my Facebook page. As expected, they were dismayed. Mom started firing off anxiety-ridden messages, asking me what was going on.

"Why aren't you talking to me?" she asked. "Why don't you come home?"

She seemed to think I had moved to New York City to be with Rocco, and that I was living with him. This made me more miffed than ever. I ignored my parents and their angsty notes. I did not want a confrontation. The chasm between us had grown too wide. I knew I hadn't shared all my troubles with them, and I knew they were terribly concerned that I had gone off to live on my own, but still, their assumptions angered and hurt me.

My parents' notes didn't stop. They seemed convinced that I was acting out because of Rocco. It disturbed me that they blamed him. He was the one helping me. He told me, "You need to see your parents. You can't have them thinking you're living with me." But I could not face them. I needed more time on my own. I still needed to figure myself out.

Rocco also encouraged me to see my sister Adele. She was living nearby, in Harlem, where she had lived for about a year working as a nurse at a hospital. It was anxiety-inducing for my parents that she had moved out on her own too. In my culture back home, you don't really move out until you're married. Adele was engaged to a wonderful man from our tribe, but they weren't living together, as that would have been frowned upon. Rocco kept telling me it would help to see Adele, to ease my way back into the family after several months of sporadic messages. Finally, I agreed.

Our meeting was awkward, as she knew I had been living in Brooklyn and had not wanted to see her. She also knew about Rocco, thanks to Facebook. One of the first things she said to me was, "Are you having sex with him?" It was exactly the kind of inquiry that had made me want to avoid my family.

"That's none of your business," I said.

"I just want you to be safe," she said.

"Thanks," I said, "but I'm not stupid."

It was a short, thorny reunion, but at least I had reconnected.

In March, Rocco drove me to Houghton College so I could visit my friends. While there, he asked me if I wanted to go to Rochester to see my parents. I said no, but I did go to see my brother Heritage on that trip. He was a pastor now, with a family of his own. As both a pastor and a protective older brother, he was a good listener. I knew I would feel comfortable with him, and I did. He didn't interrogate me or make assumptions about my life. He asked me if I was okay, and I assured him that I was. He gave me his love.

I thought it was best that Rocco not meet Heritage yet. There were just too many things going on in my life, and it didn't feel like the right time to introduce him to the family. But I showed Rocco around the city where I had grown up, and we went to the beach at Lake Ontario.

I felt so free and at ease with him, I started to breathe again, to enjoy life a little. For so long, I had been holding my breath. Now I walked outside and took deep gulps of the spring air, filling my lungs. The trees in Brooklyn were starting to bud. Soon they would burst into pink and white blossoms.

I began rebooting my life, reconnecting with groups devoted to refugees and human rights. I had let my activism slip amid my depression. One of the groups, the Women's Refugee Commission, invited me to a summit in Washington, DC, in honor of International Women's Day. I went and performed a song from my tribe in my native language. I met the queen of Belgium, Queen Mathilde, who looked young and elegant. For a moment I had an uneasy feeling, meeting the queen of the country that had once colonized my own country in Africa. But of course, that was long before her time, so I could hardly blame her for that. We had a wonderful conversation, speaking in French and discussing the importance of educating girls around the world.

I began thinking about my own education again. I looked into college for the next year.

My future came back into focus.

THIRTY

IN APRIL, MY LIFE TOOK AN INCREDIBLE TURN.
I got invited to the White House Correspondents' Dinner.
There was a chance I would get to meet President Obama
and the First Lady. In person. Face to face. The Obamas and
me—unreal.

The invitation sprang from my activism. I had become
more involved with the group RefugePoint. My friend at the
group, Sasha, asked if I would like to join him at the dinner, along with one of the group's board members, George
Lehner. I said to count me in. The evening is famous for its
flashy celebrity attendees. And of course, the Obamas.

Thus began a series of events that were surreal. First,

I was told I could pick a fabulous dress to borrow for the evening. Sasha recommended a designer named Maria Cornejo, and I went to a boutique in Manhattan lined with her elegant gowns. I invited Adele to go with me, and we had a lovely afternoon, our tensions fading. As I tried on dresses with the help of the women at the shop, I felt as if I were in a movie. The women liked a long blue gown for me, and it was stunning, but it seemed like a typical choice for such an event—too traditional, too safe. I spotted something more unique: a flowing black-and-white gown with a cool asymmetrical print.

I made the right call. When we arrived at the event, people immediately started complimenting me on the dress. Photographers snapped pictures. They said things to me like, "Show a little leg!" Bloggers came up to me. "Who are you wearing?" they asked. "Who did your makeup?" I think they thought I was an actress. They looked like they were trying to place me. They asked about my shoes, my bag. I talked with them about the outfit, and about how I was there with RefugePoint. The group had been working to resettle tens of thousands of Congolese refugees. I realized that the bloggers' interest in my dress gave me a platform to talk about the plight of refugees.

Then things got really interesting. We received a ticket

for a special greeting room, where we would meet the president and First Lady before the dinner. I couldn't believe it. Suddenly I was standing in a line of celebrities waiting to meet President Obama. The cast of *Modern Family* was there, and it was funny to hear them talking among themselves like normal people. You expect them to be like the over-the-top characters they play on TV. I spotted Gina Rodriguez, star of the show *Jane the Virgin*, and I said to her, "I think you're so cool." She was really sweet. She complimented me on my dress and got her date to snap a picture of the two of us. I handed over my cell phone, which was cracked from being dropped on the floor, and we laughed about busted-up phones.

The room was sizzling hot, and I started to sweat. I wondered why someone didn't crank up the air-conditioning. You'd think the president would rate some decent airflow.

I finally got to the front of the line. My moment had arrived. The president and First Lady greeted me warmly. Is this real? I thought. Am I seriously talking to the president? The words I had planned to say left my brain. I froze. But thankfully, the words fought their way back. I thanked President Obama for helping to resettle refugees from Congo. He said we have much more work to do in the region.

There were so many things I wanted to say. I wanted to

talk about the refugees living in camps all over the globe, displaced by war, separated from their loved ones. I wanted to talk about the massacre of my people at the camp in Gatumba and how it hardly made the news anywhere in the world. If a deadly attack like that had happened in America or Europe, you would never stop hearing about it. It pains me that the world doesn't know what happened to my tribe. I wanted to talk about the Syrian refugee crisis, and about how some people want to keep the refugees out of this country, fearing they could be terrorists. But they are just people like us, mothers and children, fleeing from conflict. They are running from the very thing we condemn: terrorism.

But I knew our time was limited, and I needed to talk to the First Lady. I turned to her and gushed, "Mrs. Obama, you're such an amazing woman. Thank you for standing up for women. Thank you for being a champion for girls' education." I was so overwhelmed, I almost cried. Here was this woman in a position of power who looks like me, a woman of such grace. Standing before her and the president, I felt a jolt of pride.

"Thank you," she said. "Tell me about yourself."

I told her about my life and my activism. And then she and I entered our own little universe, talking about education and girls' rights around the world. I was supposed to get about two minutes of time, but we must have talked for at least ten minutes. A photographer was getting antsy and asked me to turn toward the camera. President Obama waved him away and said, "Let them finish." Incredible! The president told a photographer to back off and wait for his wife and me to finish talking.

Afterward, I saw Bradley Cooper and felt emboldened to walk right up and say hello. I could not let the evening pass without speaking to him. He gave me a friendly hello and asked, "Who are you here with?" I explained about Refuge-Point, and he seemed genuinely interested. Then Sasha snapped a picture of the two of us, and Bradley told me, "By the way, you're gorgeous." I was swooning.

I also met Gabourey Sidibe, star of the film *Precious*, and we had a bonding moment. She looked at me and said, "Oh my God, I love your hair." I had pulled up my braids and worn them in a twist on top of my head, instead of straightening my hair, as black women often do for a formal event. I felt most comfortable in braids. Gabourey's father is from Senegal, and she said she loves it when black women wear their hair in traditional African styles. She said she was writing a book about black beauty, hair, and celebrity.

After the dinner, things became even more like a fairy tale. George Lehner, the RefugePoint board member, walked up to me and said, "I have something for you." It was a hand-written note, scribbled on a pamphlet, from the First Lady. George had been sitting at her table during the dinner, and she had asked him to give it to me.

The note said: *To Sandra. Keep working hard. Warmly, Michelle Obama.*

I cried. I could not believe any of this was happening.

We spent the rest of the night party-hopping. Various publications and TV networks were holding after-parties—the *Huffington Post, NBC News.* I saw more celebrities, including Chrissy Teigen and Laverne Cox. And more photographers snapped shots of me. The next day, pictures of me were splashed across the fashion pages and blogs. The *Washington Post* said, "In a sea of chiffon and florals, Sandra Uwiringiyimana's bold black-and-white graphic print by Zero + Maria Cornejo stood out."

Things were looking up. But I still had to face my family.

THIRTY-ONE

MY SISTER ADELE WAS DUE TO GET MARRIED at the end of May, and I was going to be a bridesmaid. Back home in Africa, the grandparents of her fiancé arranged to give our grandparents sixteen cows in exchange for Adele's hand in marriage, per tradition. Adele and her fiancé were planning to travel to Rwanda and hold the wedding there, just like Princesse. I was excited about going back to Africa. My parents and siblings would be there too, of course, and I knew it meant the time had come to reestablish ties.

Rocco drove me home to Rochester in early May. It was a long, somber drive. I was not looking forward to this visit, and my heart felt heavy. "It's time to make peace," Rocco told me. "You'll feel so much better once you do."

I walked up to my front door while he drove away. As soon as he left, I felt a pang. I missed him already. I walked in the house, and Mom and I just looked at each other, not speaking. I hated seeing her so upset with me, but I was annoyed with her too. Dad wasn't there, as he had already gone to Rwanda to help Adele prepare for the wedding. In the house, the air was thick with tension. Mom and I didn't speak to each other for days.

My parents lived in a suburban home on the outskirts of Rochester now, a cozy two-story house with a long dining-room table like the one back home in Africa, a big soft maroon couch to sink into, and a large-screen TV for our beloved soccer games. Framed photos from our time in America lined the living room, since the photos from our past in Africa had burned in the camp. On the top shelf of a tall cabinet, Mom kept a jug made from a hollowed-out gourd, much like the ones that she used back in the mountains of South Kivu.

More people from our tribe had been relocated now, some in Rochester. Friends and relatives came and went all day long in this home, unannounced, just like our home in Congo. Mom had begun working in a nursing home, and

Dad, as always, did everything he could to support her. He had never been physically able to return to work after being hit by the van, although he did get some disability support. I know it pained him greatly to see my mom working when he could not. Life had taken so much from him, but never his spirit. He had lived his life with such courage and grace, as had my mom. Being home reminded me of this.

After several awkward days, one of my uncles, Mutware, came over to help Mom and me talk it all out. Mutware is the generous man who had taken in my shattered family in Burundi after the massacre. He and his family had resettled in America a few years after us. For my mom and me, he became a mediator.

"I'm going to let one of you express your feelings, and then the other," he said.

It was profoundly uncomfortable for Mom and me to sit down together. There was a tsunami of emotion on both ends. I knew I hadn't explained my feelings when I had fled from college, but I didn't know how to tell her about the flashbacks and my failing grades. I just didn't think she would understand. She had always been so tenacious, no matter what life threw at her. And in my culture, it was highly unusual for parents and children to discuss their feelings, or for anyone to talk about their feelings at all. People didn't express their pain in this way. If people were having problems, they might say to pray for them, and leave it at that. Meanwhile, my mom had made assumptions about me and my life, and that had hurt me, pushing me away. We had never been further apart.

It was also the first time I had rebelled against my parents. It was the only time I had really stood up to them, and it hurt them, even though that had not been my intention. I never wanted to disobey them or cause them distress.

My mom spoke first. She listed all the ways I had messed up, starting with the way I had left school and had barely kept in touch. "How could you do that to me?" she asked. "How could you just go? If you were doing poorly in school, whatever was going on, you didn't feel like you could come to your mother and talk about it? Everyone goes through things. You don't run away." It went on for a long time.

And then it was my turn. I said, "Mom, I'm not trying to hurt you." And I finally told her everything. I told her about the flashbacks. I explained how I struggled with the fact that I had survived the massacre and Deborah had not. I said that sometimes I blamed myself for her death, and I felt that my parents blamed me for her death. I told her how it disturbed me when she referred to me as the youngest in the family, as if Deborah had not existed. And I told her it bothered me how none of us ever talked about Deborah. The truth came tumbling out. I said things I had never said to her before.

I wasn't expecting Mom to understand or agree with everything I said, but I was determined to tell her. I needed to stand my ground, to be myself, whether my parents could relate to where I was coming from or not. My time in Brooklyn had become a defining moment for me. I was becoming my own person—a different person from the one my parents had expected me to be. But at the same time, my parents were the ones who had instilled the confidence in me to be myself. I pointed this out to my mom. I also told her that I knew American culture terrified her because she was not familiar with it. She had not grown up with it. I told her that I understood this.

"Everything will be okay," I assured her. "I would never abandon my principles or ideals." I explained that I was learning to see the world through a broader lens.

"I just want to live my life," I said.

My mom listened. We had never spoken so intimately.

"When are you going back to college?" she asked.

Education meant so much to her, and she didn't want me to blow up the opportunities that she had worked hard to provide for me. She and my dad had made so many sacrifices for their children. I understood that. I told her I was looking into different schools, including one in New York City called Mercy College. She wanted me to go back to Houghton College, which was much closer to Rochester. She didn't like the idea of my living in the city. But I had fallen in love with the city—its creative energy, its mix of diverse cultures. I was liberated there, surrounded by people from all over the planet. There's a certain sense of camaraderie in the city, a feeling that we're all in it together, no matter how different we might be.

Mom also asked about Rocco, as I knew she would. I told her he's a great guy, a caring and supportive soul who had spurred me to reunite with my family. I explained how I had met him and assured her that I was not living with him, as she had assumed. She shook her head and said, "You are not going to marry him."

"Mom, I'm not getting married."

"Then what are you doing?" she asked. Dating was not part of her life experience.

"Mom," I implored, "I don't think it's fair for you to expect me to live within these cultural expectations. I'm not trying to spite you. But we live in America now. I don't want to live my life based on where I came from. I don't want to be defined by a race, a culture, a tribe."

I explained that I deeply love and respect my tribe and

my culture. I told her, "If I marry someone from my culture, that would be awesome. But if I marry someone from outside my culture, that would be awesome too."

She stared at me intently. She could see that I was not going to budge. Even if we did not agree with each other on that day, we began to get to know each other on a new level. We knew we had only just begun talking.

THIRTY-TWO

IN LATE MAY, MY PARENTS, SIBLINGS, AND I all came together in Rwanda for Adele's wedding. It was the first time I had seen my father since I had left college amid my breakdown, and I was nervous. But when our eyes met, I knew everything would be fine. He just looked happy to see me. When my dad is in Africa, he looks peaceful, restored. Africa is his true home. And I always knew that I had his support, no matter what. We had been through so much together, my dad and me. On that visit, my family and I relaxed and shared some laughs. My siblings teased me about "finding myself."

"You're so Americanized," they said. "You're finding yourself? When did you lose yourself?"

It was a joyous time as we prepared for Adele's wedding. We went on a safari for the first time, like tourists. The hot African sun felt good on my skin after the long winter in New York, and we gawked at hippos, rhinos, giraffes, and zebras. For the wedding, Princesse and I were bridesmaids and wore gorgeous rose-colored gowns. Adele was married on a hilltop, with a view of Kigali stretching out below, a stunning backdrop of red roofs and green hills. I stayed in Rwanda for three months, and I loved it.

After I returned home, something beautiful happened: Mom and I began to grow closer than we had ever been. Gradually, we started talking more, confiding in each other and expressing ourselves in ways we never had. She opened up to me, talking about her feelings and worries—something she had not done in the past. Mom had always been the strong and stoic one, carrying the family on her shoulders. She began to realize that it's okay to express yourself. It doesn't mean you're weak.

It's a realization that helped me in my journey as well. I felt so much better when I let my feelings out, instead of trying to keep them bottled up. It's exhausting when you think that you're not entitled to your emotions. I began talking to my mom more about my problems and issues too, and she listened. She gave me a piece of advice that I have come to love: "Be righteous and faithful when no one is watching." I like that message a lot. No matter what challenges you face in life, you can focus on being a good person. It's how my mom always lived her own life, with such dignity and faith in God.

As for my own feelings about God, they continue to evolve. I find it comforting to pray, and to put my faith in him. But I have many questions still. Our relationship remains a work in progress.

After I made up with my parents, my brothers and sisters began to open up to me in new ways as well, talking about their challenges and concerns. This was a new development for all of us. My siblings had seen me at my worst, and they had seen how I felt better when I expressed myself honestly and openly. As it turned out, my breakdown had become a breakthrough for my family. While it was a very difficult experience for me to be at odds with my family for all those months, I'm glad I went off on my own to figure things out for myself.

I spent the summer in Rochester with my parents. I applied and was accepted to Mercy College in New York City for the fall. I planned to study international relations.

I looked forward to moving ahead with my life and my studies in the city. I talked to my various human rights and refugee groups about ways I could get more involved in the future. Visiting the refugee camp in Rwanda with my sisters had helped me feel more driven than ever to help give forgotten people a voice.

Around this time, another gratifying thing happened too. Some of the men from my tribe began to warm up to me. Instead of being concerned that a young woman was speaking for the community, they saw that I was developing a voice that could help people understand our experience. Some of the men approached me personally, saying, "Hey, congratulations. We are so proud of you." An uncle told me that he wished more men in the community would encourage their daughters to be like me. It meant so much to hear it.

As I mended ties with my family and prepared for college, Rocco and I continued to talk, but the distance began to take its toll. Over the summer months spent apart from each other, we drifted. We had met at just the right time for both of us—a time when we were lost, struggling to figure out our lives. Our relationship had been an escape from reality, a little utopia. But now, as we were stepping back into reality and moving forward with our lives, it became difficult to focus on the relationship. We had trouble seeing a future together.

I wanted to get my life back on track, and he wanted to do the same. One day, we had a deep, heart-wrenching conversation, and decided that our relationship had run its course.

I knew it was right for us to move on. Still, I couldn't help but feel devastated. I cried for days. He had meant so much to me at such an important time in my life. It pained me to think he would fade into my past. I also knew that my family would have had a hard time accepting him because he was not from my culture, and there would have been a lot of anxiety for everyone. But that's not why we broke up. And I don't blame my parents for their views. They want the best for me, and the way they see it, a man from my tribe would be best for me. It's how they grew up, and it's what they know.

I, however, have come to realize that I want to live my life with my heart and mind open to other people, other cultures, other tribes. I don't want to stop myself from developing relationships with people because of their race or culture or where they come from. I want to appreciate people for who they are, not for the color of their skin. I want to be inclusive.

I know now that I want to live freely, without separating myself from others, without feeling that I need to pick a side, to stick to my own. After all, if people remain divided and closed off from different cultures, it can lead to the kind of extreme thinking that took Deborah's life. Back then, my people were seen as different—that is why we were targeted. We looked different. We sounded different. And so people wanted to wipe us out with their machetes and guns.

What kind of justice would it be for Deborah if I embraced the very notions of division that killed her? My life has been a journey to come to this realization. As a child, I witnessed the unthinkable: I saw my sister murdered before my eyes because of discrimination and hate. But I have learned that if we want to change the world, we can't harden our hearts and shut ourselves off from other cultures. We must open up our hearts. We must not fall prey to the kind of thinking that separates us. Yes, you can appreciate your history and your culture. You can embrace it. But you can embrace other cultures too. And, yes, you can be angry and seek justice when you are attacked. I want the killers who targeted my people to face justice. But going forward, I don't want to spread the seeds of separation. I want to open myself to people of all races, cultures, and faiths.

Ultimately, it is the lesson Deborah has taught me. This book is for her. If I could sit down with her today, this is the story I would tell her. Deborah is with me still, and always will be. Sometimes at night, I talk with her in my dreams.

When I see her there, she is always six years old.

AUTHOR'S NOTE

Life seemed to stop for me after the Gatumba Massacre. I lived every day terrified of what had happened that night. Even now, I still relive the worst night of my life, long after the world has stopped caring. I heard a man, Agathon Rwasa, go on public radio and confess to having killed my sweet sister along with 165 other people. And then he went on to run for president of Burundi. As I watched the world continue to spin, I stood there wondering what I had done for God to grant me such a life. I wondered why I stayed, while others did not. I stood numb year after year. I heard the deafening silence of the whole world. I was waiting for someone to tell me that I mattered.

I wrote this book because I was tired of outsiders always writing my history, my present, and my future. I have spent my life being just statistics in pages talking about how many of Congo's children are hungry, out of school, or are living in conflict. I was tired of simply existing between the lines of articles and books that were written by people who had never met me and knew very little of what it was like to be me.

I wrote *How Dare the Sun Rise* to tell my story, Deborah's story, and the stories of the millions of people who feel invisible. I refuse to let the lives that were lost in Gatumba be forgotten. I refuse to stop seeking justice. I refuse to be silenced. Even with my last breath, I will seek justice for Gatumba.

How Dare the Sun Rise is a testament to the failure of Agathon Rwasa and FNL. These men have ended the lives of 166 people, but they started a fire in me. As long as I am still alive, they have failed. As long as people hear my story, they have failed. As long as I keep fighting, they have failed! This book is a declaration of my independence. It is a story of how hatred failed and love and justice prevailed. My hope is that my story serves as inspiration for those who have been harmed by the very institutions that were meant to protect them. There is power in our voices. The more of us speak up, the more likely we are to be heard. Our communities cannot thrive if some of us are made to feel like we do not matter. I hope this book inspires more people to stand up for the voiceless. Don't let your silence be another person's death. Fighting for each other is the only way we all win.

INFORMATION AND RESOURCES

If you'd like to learn more about some of the issues regarding women, refugees, and poverty that I discuss in the book, please visit and help these organizations. All three of these groups are doing amazing work and deserve your support.

Jimbere Fund is a nonprofit organization founded by myself, my sister Adele Kibasumba, and her husband, Obadias Ndaba. Our mission at Jimbere Fund is to revitalize distressed communities in rural Congo. We work with Congo's most remote populations to design and implement individualized high-impact development interventions that expand opportunities and access to critical services, create jobs, and lift people out of poverty in a sustainable way. Our approach blends community organizing and development interventions. Communities identify their most pressing needs in education, women's empowerment, health, and agricultural productivity, and we work with them to find solutions and co-implement them.

How can you help? Here are four ways to support:

- Donate on our website at Jimberefund.org. This will mean a lot and enable us to continue our work.
- Stay in touch via newsletter and/or social media, and spread the word to your networks.
- Invite us to talk at your events and to your networks.
- Introduce us to people/contacts/organizations who might be interested in supporting our mission.

Maman Shujaa means "Hero Women" in Swahili. The Maman Shujaa are a women's movement in the Democratic Republic of Congo, a movement for peace, women's rights, rights of the indigenous, and for communities and nature. The Maman Shujaa are enabling women and girls with free computer training and online access to advocate or blog their stories; with programs that employ and empower them in environmental conservation and industry, making washable, reusable sani-pads; programs that mentor, equip, and enable the next generation of Maman Shujaa through their Girl Ambassadors for Peace. Learn more at www.herowomenrising.org.

The humanitarian organization RefugePoint has helped me and tens of thousands of other refugees in life-threatening situations find safety and rebuild our lives. RefugePoint was founded in 2005 to provide lasting solutions for the world's most vulnerable refugees—especially women, children, and urban refugees. Through resettlement and holistic services that promote stabilization and self-reliance, RefugePoint identifies and protects refugees who have no other options for survival. RefugePoint envisions a future in which refugees are able to move from exclusion to inclusion, and from dependence to self-reliance. To learn more about RefugePoint and to donate, visit www.refugepoint.org.

ACKNOWLEDGMENTS

Thank you to my parents, Prudence and Rachel, for investing in me when the world around you told you otherwise.

Thank you to my sisters Princesse, Adele, and Claudine for always leading by example and challenging me to be the best me that I can be.

Thank you to my brothers, Heritage, Chris, and Alex, for always having my back.

Thank you to my whole family for letting me share our intimate stories with the world.

Thank you to Abby for always treating my story with respect and dignity.

Thank you to my agent, Jessica, and my editor, Ben, for

recognizing the need for stories like mine.

Thank you to Francisco for being my rock.

Thank you to Tina Brown and Women in the World for giving me the space to share my story with the world.

Thank you to Sasha Chanoff for working and fighting for people like me.

Thank you to Mercy High School for Young Women for giving me an excellent educational foundation.

Thank you to New Hope Free Methodist Church for welcoming my family as your own.

Thank you to Kayce Freed Jennings for being my friend and support system when I had none.

Thank you to Joanna Heatwole for the incalculable things that you've done for my family and me.

Thank you to the "Survivors" exhibit participants for letting me tell your stories and Visual Studies Workshop for giving the platform to share those stories with the world.

Thank you to all the friends, pastors, and educators whose encouragement and love helped me grow in to who I am today, including Kaya Hesed Stratton, Shannon Crammer, Philip Maenza, Linda Adams, pastor Michael and Amelia Traylor, Leah Rusin, Virginia Lenyk, Mabel Hope, Neema Namadamu, Ms. Clasquin, Suzanne Johnson, Felix Mwungeri, Kate Fady, Colleen and Nina Glass, Elizabeth Primus,

Keri Barnett Basset, Kim Barker, Rita Fancher, Mr. DeSain, Ms. Khoji, Mutware Makuza.

—Sandra

Thank you to Sandra for sharing her story.

Thank you to my creative and ever supportive family: John Pesta, an author who taught me the art of storytelling, Maureen O'Hara Pesta, an artist who sees the world in a different light, and Jesse Pesta, a globe-trotting writer, photographer, and an editor at the *New York Times*.

Thank you to my agent, Jess Regel, and my editor, Ben Rosenthal, and to Katherine Tegen and her team at Harper-Collins, for seeing the beauty in this book.

A special thanks to Joanna Coles, an inspiration to journalists everywhere who aspire to think creatively.

Thank you to Tina Brown and her team at Women in the World, including Kyle Gibson, Anna Hall, and Karen Compton, for introducing me to Sandra.

Thank you to authors Sheila Weller, Sam Marshall, and Laurie Sandell for their stellar advice on all things publishing.

Many thanks to all the editors who have helped me tell great stories, including Kayla Adler, Miriam Arond, Sara Austin, Lauren Smith Brody, Laura Brounstein, Alison Brower, Joyce Chang, Katie Connor, Riza Cruz, Pip Cummings, Roe

D'Angelo, Deidre Depke, Mike Elek, Rosemary Ellis, Edward Felsenthal, Lori Fradkin, Anne Fulenwider, Lea Goldman, Susan Goodall, Jill Herzig, Noelle Howey, Lauren Iannotti, Susy Jackson, Rich Jaroslovsky, Whitney Joiner, Ellen Kampinsky, Lucy Kaylin, Marina Khidekel, Cindi Leive, Ellen Levine, Tracy Middleton, Marty Munson, Wendy Naugle, Jessica Pels, Geraldine Sealey, Michele Shapiro, Harry Siegel, Jane Spencer, Paul Steiger, Sade Strehlke, Andrew Tavani, Tunku Varadarajan, Tom Weber, and Leslie Yazel, among many others.

—Abby

SANDRA UWIRINGIYIMANA is cofounder and director of partnerships & communications at Jimbere Fund, an organization that aims to revitalize distressed communities in Congo by investing in women. Since her family's resettlement in 2007, Sandra has fought hard to call for justice for the Gatumba massacre and has become a voice for women and girls, refugees and immigrants, and forgotten people like the Banyamulenge tribe. In telling her story, Sandra has shared the world stage with Angelina Jolie, Hillary Clinton, and Tina Brown at the Women in the World Summit. She addressed the United Nations Security Council at the request of Ambassador Samantha Power to plead with world leaders to act on the pressing issue of children in armed conflict. Sandra is finishing her studies in New York City.

ABIGAIL PESTA is an award-winning journalist who has lived and worked around the world, from New York to London to Hong Kong. Her investigative and feature reporting has appeared in global publications, including *Cosmopolitan*, the *New York Times, Marie Claire,* the *Wall Street Journal, Newsweek, Glamour,* the *Atlantic, New York* magazine, and many others.